Robinson Public Library District
606 N. Jefferson Street
Robinson, IL 62454

Single Parent Secrets:

How to Master Solo Parenting
&
Raise Amazing Children

Yolandra Drake, RN, BSN

This book is designed to provide information and motivation to our readers. It is sold with the understanding that the publisher is not engaged to render any type of psychological, legal, or any other kind of professional advice. The content in this book is the sole expression and opinion of its author, and not necessarily that of the publisher. Neither the publisher nor the individual author(s) shall be liable for any physical, psychological, emotional, financial, or commercial damages, including, but not limited to, special, incidental, consequential or other damages. You are responsible for your own choices, actions, and results.

All rights reserved. This book or any portion thereof may not be reproduced, stored, transmitted in any form or used in any manner whatsoever without the prior express written permission of the author/publisher except for use of brief quotations in a book review.

Copyright © 2015 by Yolandra Drake. All rights reserved
Published by Yolah Media, Houston, TX

To my father Edward Drake Sr., gone too soon at the age of 56. I miss him so much every day. I am grateful for and love the relationship that blossomed between he and my daughter for the short time they had together. Much love ☺!

TABLE OF CONTENTS:

Introduction......7

ASPECTS OF SINGLE PARENTING

Secret #1: Single Parents Rock! 11
Secret #2: May the Real Single Parents Stand Up! 33
Secret #3: Single Parents are Superheroes! 40
Secret #4: Single Parents are Strong and Courageous! (Includes My Journey to Single Parenthood)......51
Secret #5: Sacrifices are Doubly Essential for Single Parents......67

SINGLE PARENT SURVIVAL SECRETS

Secret #6: God Loves Single Parents and Their Children......74
Secret #7: It Really Does Take a Village to Raise a Child......86
Secret #8: Create and Cherish Memories with Your Children......101
Secret #9: Supreme Self-Care is Critical......108

Secret #10: To Date or Not to Date: A Choice to Make as a Single Parent......118

Secret #11: Single parents CAN be financially responsible AND healthy! 127

SECRETS TO RAISING CHILDREN WHO THRIVE
"Children are PRECIOUS Gifts from GOD"

Secret #12: A Child's Needs are Truly Simple, But We Make it Complicated......144

Secret #13: Children Provide the Supreme Gift of Unconditional Love, if We Just Allow Them......154

COMMUNICATION SECRETS

Secret #14: "Do as I say, not as I do" Does Not Work! 161

Secret #15: Openness and Honesty in Communication Builds Trust with Children......169

BEHAVIOR & DISCIPLINE
"Our job is to train up a child in the way they should go"
| Proverbs 22:6

Secret #16: Kids Behaving Badly is Universal......181

Secret #17: Either You Teach Your Children—or the World Will Teach Them......186

Secret #18: Children Depend on You for Age-Appropriate Discipline......193

EDUCATION

Secret #19: Love and Appreciation of School/Education Starts at Home with the Parent......232

Secret #20: Single Parents Wear Many Hats......251

Conclusion......260

INTRODUCTION

Wouldn't it be wonderful if all children came with instruction manuals? I remember my mother always saying, "I knew nothing about raising children; they were not born with instruction books. I did the best I could." Fast-forward about 40 years and now there is a multitude of parenting instruction books available. Even just 20 years ago when I gave birth to my daughter, there were not nearly as many. When addressing single parenting and our unique challenges, the number of parenting books dwindled even further as I perused various library shelves and bookstores.

I feel as if I have been purposed to write this book. It has been in my heart for a while, at least 15 years, and I am grateful that I have finally made the time to get it completed. This is especially true being a single parent, as time is such a rarity. All the experiences I have had raising my daughter are not to keep to myself; I feel it is my duty to share my journey as a single parent, being as transparent as possible so that I may inspire someone else.

There are a few things I hope to accomplish in writing this book. First, I want to confirm that it is possible to *defy a*nd completely disrupt the prevailing condescending and non-motivating stigmas that distort the image of single parents (especially single moms and their children) as dysfunctional by-products of society. We don't have to succumb to these! I want to demonstrate how children of single parent households can be just as (or even more) successful than children of traditional two parent households –even with increased challenges. It is more difficult, but it is possible. We've just got to put in the work.

Secondly, I want to share my success as an ordinary middle-class mother raising a daughter alone. I want to share my tenacity and victories in beating the odds, as well as disclose my gaffes/mistakes in hopes that I may support someone else in a resourceful way. You don't have to make the same mistakes I did.

Lastly, it can be frightening when you become a single parent, depending on your circumstances and your journey to becoming one. There is so much you do not know, but wish you knew. You have no idea where to gather the knowledge that you need to successfully parent, and then add to the mix being a solo parent, doing it all alone. No matter how many friends' or family members' kids you babysit, they can never prepare you for the experience of being a single parent, which is always a full-time job.

I searched high and low for tangible tips and solutions to help me master solo parenting. If I knew back then what I know now, it would have made my life so much easier, my daughter's life so much richer, and I would not have made some of the mistakes I did. I would have made wiser choices for myself, as well as for my daughter. I wrote this book for others in similar single parenting situations so I could share the top twenty secrets or "tips" I discovered that were essential to mastering and being successful at solo parenting.

I want anyone reading this book to know that you are not alone. It is not easy but you can do it! As the popular truism states, "Take what you like and leave the rest." No single book can address everything for everybody, but my hope is you will discover many nuggets you can utilize that are valuable and applicable to your personal life scenario and assist you on your journey to becoming the single parent you want to be. If you are ready to make a positive change, you will find this information helpful and meaningful to ensure you make the transition into being the best single parent you can be, and the one your child/children deserve.

I have learned a lot from being a single parent. I have experienced many triumphs and successes. It has been a journey getting through my daughter's childhood and helping her enter young adulthood as a happy, confident, intelligent young woman, graduating high school as an honor student, cum laude in the top 15% of her class, with great friends, no drinking, no drugs, no smoking, no sex, no pregnancies, and now (when I first started writing this book) beginning her freshman year in college. Wow! I think I did well and so does she, being the end result of *mastering solo parenting and raising an amazing child who thrives*!

There are various challenges you are faced with as a single parent and each circumstance varies in so many ways. In this book, I provide the hindsight wisdom and secrets I attained along the way so that maybe your journey, although unique but similar in so many ways, may be more successful. I will provide you with the highlights of my voyage so we can all get it right and create a new and improved, positive, strong image about single parents and our offspring. So let's get started!

(SECRET #1) SINGLE PARENTS ROCK!

Why would anyone choose to be a single parent? Being a single parent is extremely tough and is plagued with a plethora of negative stereotypes. There are such low expectations of children raised in single parent households and extra negativity about single moms especially, as if they are the scum of the earth.

Yet one-third of American children—a total of 15 million!—are being raised by single moms. The number of single parent homes has nearly doubled since 1960 according to the 2010-2012 Statistical Abstract by the U.S. Census Bureau. 72.6% of single parents are mothers; among this percentage, 45% are divorced or separated, 1.7% widowed, and 34% are single moms who never married.

Single parent households are associated with a high incidence of poverty and are often seen as doomed for failure. According to the 2012 U.S. Census Bureau, half of single mother families had an annual income of less than $25,000. The median income for single mother families ($25,353) is only one-third the median for families of married couples ($78,699).

Single parenting is crippled with negative, brutally advertised stigmas and media propaganda, not to mention extremely low statistics regarding success rates. Single moms get a bad rap, but even more so, children of single mothers are immediately plagued as low achievers, "bad kids" and troublemakers who are usually involved with drugs, alcohol, gangs, violent crimes and imprisonment; the list goes on.

The female children of single mothers, especially those with low incomes, are boldly labeled as promiscuous, with early pregnancy rates, dependency on welfare, and are overall seen as just low-class and trashy. These children of single parent households are stereotyped in any negative way possible.

Other negative statistics include:

• According to 2010 U.S. Census data: one-third of American children – a total of 15 million – are being raised without a father. This number has doubled since 1960.

• **Fatherless children** are at a dramatically greater risk of drug and alcohol abuse, mental illness, suicide, poor educational performance, teen pregnancy, and criminality.

- **Poverty:** Children living in single parent homes without fathers are more likely to grow up in poverty. Married couples with children have an average income of $80,000, while single mothers average only $24,000.

- **Criminal Activity/Prison:** More than one half of all youths incarcerated for criminal acts lived in one-parent families when they were children. (Children's Defense Fund)

- **Teen Pregnancy:** 75% of teenage pregnancies are adolescents from single parent homes. (Children in Need: Investment Strategies - Committee for Economic Development)

- **Suicides:** 63% of suicides are individuals from single parent families. (FBI Law Enforcement Bulletin - Investigative Aid)

- **Sexual activity:** A large study of 700 adolescents concluded that adolescents from single parent households engage in greater and earlier sexual activity as compared to adolescents in two parent households.

- **Drug Use/Drinking Problems:** Studies have

shown, when there is an absence of a father in the household, it adversely affects the behavior of children and they have a greater likelihood of marijuana and alcohol usage when compared to children raised in two parent homes.

- 75% of children/adolescents in chemical dependency hospitals are from single parent families. (Center for Disease Control, Atlanta, GA)

- Teenagers living in single parent households are more likely to abuse alcohol and at an earlier age compared to children reared in two parent households.

- Children in single parent families are nearly twice as likely to drop out of school as children from two parent families.

These are just a few of thousands of prevailing negative facts found on the internet alone. I was blown away as I researched the common statistics out there, which also nowadays translate into perceived norms and truths to those that are hyper judgmental of single parent families, especially single moms. I strongly felt and knew they were not reflective of my world and household, and the households of other friends of mine who were single parents. These statistics and beliefs are what contribute to the negative labeling correlated with single parents and their children and the low expectations that some begin to accept and own as their destiny.

With such a high statistical failure rate, why would anyone choose to be a single parent with so much perceived doom and poor levels of success? The real truth, in spite of all this negativity, and the secret that I have learned is that SINGLE PARENTS ROCK! If I had paid much attention to this when I first became a single parent, I would have thought I was predestined for failure like so many young moms today tend to believe after this has been programmed into their psyche. The prevailing perception of critics becomes their reality. I am grateful that I initially had no idea about these statistics and stereotypes, not that I would have chosen to believe them, but just because life is difficult enough without having self-limiting, self-defeating beliefs to distract you. When I initially became a single parent, I didn't have any positive single parent role models that I could identify with to inspire me upon starting this journey.

Single Parents and Our Children Receive a Lot of Blame

In the second debate of the 2012 Presidential election, candidate Mitt Romney made a comment that was extremely offensive and derogatory to single parent families. When asked about his opinion on gun control and the assault weapons ban, he brought up the issue of marriage seemingly at random—with this condescending response to the question: "Gosh, to tell our kids that before they have babies, they ought to think about getting married to someone—that's a great idea because if there's a two parent family, the prospect of living in poverty goes down dramatically. The opportunities that the child will be able to achieve increase dramatically."

So now single parents are to blame for gun violence? This was the message that many walked away with after hearing his statements. Single parents constantly get the blame for society's ills. Why? Because women head most single parent households.

I was actually watching this debate at the time this statement (among others) was made and was flabbergasted when I heard this. It was disheartening on a few levels.

The first being that Mr. Romney's statement certainly makes it seem as though middle or low-income individuals who happen to be single parents have no common sense, intelligence or moral character. That we are not teaching our kids that they should be married before having children or about the importance of family and households with a husband and a wife. He also implied that the breakdown of the family (or more specifically single parenting households) leads to poverty, which automatically equates to violence.

Violence is a universal issue, not just a low income or poverty-ridden behavior of single parent households. Even the 2001 Surgeon General Report concluded there is no one factor that can predict the likelihood that a child will grow up to be violent. It happens in any family structure and is not motivated by any particular one. The gun violence situation has plenty to do with who has access to these weapons that are killing innocent people, young and old, which includes gang violence and mass killings of people in theatres, schools, retail stores, etc.

Gun violence has plenty to do with the drug epidemic that has been running rampant in our country since the 1980s and has been destroying families and affecting all households in some capacity, not just single parent households. Gun violence has more to do with gun control than single parent family control, dealing with mental health issues and policies, police control and criminal defense measures and laws, and dealing with and controlling the drug epidemic that is plaguing our country. It has to do with not allowing violent and mentally ill people to have access to guns or the ability to purchase guns, and having stronger sanctions and regulations.

There are rampant statements like these you hear in speeches and read on the Internet regarding single parents and their offspring, substantiating the fact that there are so many people in America who are judgmental, close-minded and/or have hateful attitudes towards others that are different in *any* way. These grumblers and their thinking is so disconnected from the realities of the world and they have no real clue about the complexities that lower and/or middle-income families and their children experience in day-to-day life, let alone single parents. Everyone is unique; every family dynamic is unique, even every single parent family household dynamic is unique, but critics always want to lump everyone into the same category without considering their situation. Listening to politicians and the media, the single parent family has long been used as a scapegoat for our society's shortcomings.

There are many people in society today who are unwilling to accept change and don't want to accept the fact that the status quo nuclear family is ever changing for various reasons. Instead of trying to comprehend and support the changes that are sometimes truly inevitable, they battle against it, become extremely judgmental, hostile, derogatory and cruel. This is not to take away from the stable, nuclear, two parent family that I believe is ideal for children. But sometimes this ideal situation is just not possible, and these are the instances where change will surface. No matter what…change is happening. The nuclear family is changing and we have to embrace it, try to fix what is not working and move on to support all of our people, our children, our communities and our country, because we are all interconnected. We are one country and others in our communities will affect us all either negatively or positively at some point in our lives.

A major fact to note is that single parent families are succeeding and doing so in large numbers, contrary to popular belief. Children in single parent families can thrive and do just as well as in other family structures, except they have to do it in a more stressful and challenging manner because they are constantly faced with stigmas and negativity from outside social, political and legal entities that penalize and work against them (along with the already-apparent challenges of growing up with only one parent). It is evident that these nagging stigmas are designed to work against single parent families in order to justify social policies and legislation that are damaging and punitive, designed to support failure. But who suffers the most as a result? Single parents suffer, but the children suffer the most. What is missed throughout this is the fact that these tragic events create a boomerang effect where our society will also suffer because these children will grow up and become citizens, neighbors, products of our society and communities, and we all will be affected.

I could go on and on, but let me share a few more interesting statistics from the most recent U.S. Census Bureau: 84% of the custodial single parents are mothers and 16% are fathers. Among the mothers who are single parents, 79% were employed and 49.9% worked full-time while 29.7% worked part-time. Of the single fathers, 90% were employed, with 71.7% working full-time and 18.4%

working part-time. Among the custodial mothers in the U.S., about 22% received Medicaid, 23.3% received food stamps and 12% received public housing or rent subsidy assistance, and 5% received Temporary Assistance for Needy Families.

Myths vs. Facts about Single Parent Life

I found these statistics interesting because one of the biggest myths people are led to believe is that single mothers are basically poor, career welfare recipients. The above statistics represent less than half of all single mothers. The majority of myths and negative statistics usually portrayed imply that a vast majority of single parents are on welfare and government assistance. The fact is, this is simply not true. There are many single parents gainfully employed, in business for themselves, working hard, taking care of and providing for their children without government assistance. This equates to the simple truth that the majority of single parents are not on government assistance. Most single parent households are thriving and raising phenomenal children.

Are some single parents abusing the welfare system?

Yes, some are; this fact cannot be denied. There are also married couples abusing the welfare system, as well as the IRS system and many other government, political and financial systems. Let me clarify: I was never on welfare and worked extremely hard to support my daughter and myself independently, and unfortunately, even without child support as many other single parents have done. I do not and will never advocate abuse of the welfare system, government system or any other system although it is done all of the time, even by the wealthy.

There will always be people abusing systems: politics, power, position, people, relationships, etc. When the system is being abused it obviously means that the system is broken and not functioning as intended. There are a lot of good people out there who really need assistance short-term; don't punish these people who need legitimate help. Somebody needs to fix all of the systems and not just focus on this one.

The society we live in is so afraid of anything that is different or doesn't fit into a specific mold of what is acceptable. Those in society quickly judge and demonize anything or anyone different because they don't understand it or care to…until it shows up on their staircase, knocks on their backdoor, moves in and takes shelter while staring back at them in the mirror. As I stated earlier, myths are rampant, but the truth that is not broadcasted and has been kept a secret for too long is that SINGLE PARENTS ROCK! Single parents are extraordinary, courageous, capable, strong, resourceful, resilient, determined, successful, and great at overcoming obstacles. They have stamina, drive, fortitude, and exceptional leadership abilities!

In opposition to the myths are facts and real-life examples to debunk these negative stigmas about children from single parent households being underachievers, sociopaths and anything associated with negativity in society. There are so many successful people in the public eye who were raised by single parents, but many are oblivious to this because it goes unmentioned until they make a mistake as we all do at times. Then, it is pointed out that "this person was raised by a single parent" in such a manner as to blame this status for their mistake or demise. Some of the successful people raised in single parent households are historical figures who I was surprised to learn about during my research. Let's look at some positive facts about people who were raised by Single parents that Rock!

Single Parents Who Raised Superstars

A single parent raised President George Washington after his father died when he was eleven years old, and he later became our first president of the United States. A single mother raised Thomas Jefferson, our third president, after his father died when he was ten years old. A single mother with the help of his grandparents raised our 42nd president, Bill Clinton, after his father died in a car crash prior to his birth. His mother remarried when he was four, but was later divorced when President Clinton was about 14 years old, due to his stepfather's alcoholism and abusive behavior, according to biography.com.

A single parent raised our 44th and current president, Barack Obama, after his father left when he was about two years old. His mother later remarried temporarily and he spent a lot of time with his maternal grandparents.

There are also many successful entertainers who were raised by single parents. Oprah Winfrey was raised by a single parent. Although her childhood was extremely challenging to say the least, and plagued with abuse and suffering, she still rose to be the most successful television talk show host and one of the richest people in America. She is the first African American female billionaire, and in 2010, became the richest self-made woman in America and has a myriad of astounding accomplishments throughout her career. Do your thing, Oprah!

A single mother raised actor, songwriter, musician and dancer Usher. I recently learned from watching Oprah's *Next Chapter* that Usher's stepfather gave his mother an ultimatum to either choose him or her son and of course she chose her son and helped him to become a highly successful and well-known singer, songwriter, performer and businessman.

Dwayne Wade, a successful three-time NBA champion with the Miami Heat, was raised by a single parent who happened to be his grandmother (his mother was addicted to drugs). LeBron James, the nine-time NBA All-Star and NBA Champion with the Miami Heat, was raised by a single parent who realized she needed assistance and allowed him to later live with the Walker family that could provide more stability and guidance. A single parent raised Gabrielle Douglas, the first African American gymnast in Olympic history to become the individual all-around gold medalist as well as the only American all-around champion to win multiple gold medals. Other athletes include Kevin Durant, Shaquille O'Neal, Warrick Dunn, Michael Phelps and Jackie Robinson, among countless others.

The list of successful people in America raised by single parents goes on and on: Ursula Burns (CEO of Xerox), Ed Bradley (CBS TV news correspondent and Editor of 60 Minutes). Hollywood actors and celebrities: Halle Berry, Matt LeBlanc, Julia Roberts, Tom Cruise, Angelina Jolie, Martin Lawrence, Audrey Hepburn, and the late Bernie Mac. Musicians, songwriters and business moguls: Sean "P. Diddy" Combs, Kanye West, Jay-Z, Justin Bieber, Alicia Keys, Kelly Rowland, Mariah Carey, and again the list goes on and on!

These are examples of people who had a passion and a strong desire for success by any means necessary and did not let anything stop them from achieving their God-given greatness instilled in them. A parent, grandparent, mentor, teacher or coach inspired them. These extraordinary people worked hard and did not let their single parent household status or the negative perceptions of the world they inhabit influence their destiny for greatness.

There are many more examples of successful Americans raised by single parents who go on to do exceptional things. These people defied odds and broke the barriers in spite of their circumstances, whether in the public eye or not, and I am sure that many of us know them personally.

Don't get me wrong: I believe that, if possible, children need two loving parents in their lives. I believe in the institution of marriage and having a strong, stable, loving and healthy two parent household where kids can thrive. But this household may not always be available. It takes courage to know when it is time to walk away from a destructive relationship that is detrimental to both the parent and the child. The household needs to be healthy, whether it has one or two parents.

I have learned from experience that it is impossible for one parent to take the place of two and provide your child with all they need. I personally have tried and had an enormous desire to be all things, but I learned and disappointingly accepted the fact that there was no way that I, as a mom, could ever replace what was missing from an absent father in my daughter's life.

Sometimes I would jokingly say, "I am the mother

and the father," but my daughter would laugh it off and cutely say, "Mom, you are not a man, you can't be a dad." She did not want to accept that I was both mother and father and took it literally in a physical gender-based manner, but I was meaning it literally because I was doing it all. Many times I have watched her wish and long for what only a dad could provide her emotionally, spiritually, mentally and physically. There will always be something missing for her, a void deep within that I can never fulfill as a mother.

It has given me much agony and grief over the years to know that no matter what, the love and attention of a father was something that I could never supply. Boys need their fathers to teach them how to be a man and show him what he will look like when he gets older. Girls need their fathers to help them feel beautiful, worthy, accepted and loved for who they are; to teach them what to expect and how to be treated by men among so many other things.

I grew up with my father in a two parent household and knew how great that was (the many benefits and experiences) and I longed for her to have that experience. I knew this life experience was something she would never have with an absent father. I could provide much, but this was the one major need that I could not provide for her no matter how creatively I tried. It was impossible, and that was heartbreaking to finally accept, but there was nothing I could do. I was powerless in making her dad show up and be a dad.

As a parent you want your children to be joyful, have a complete life and grow up strong and secure. You want to give them the world, want the best for them in every way, but eventually you have to accept the fact that there are some things you just cannot give them that they should have, and this awareness can be distressing to swallow and digest. It is best to accept this and move on while trying to provide them with the best of you that you can. Sometimes you have little control of the situation but it is important to accept that "it is what it is" and move on to greatness.

There is plenty of research proving that the advantages children obtain from living in two parent families may actually be due to family stability, more than the fact that their parents are married. It is being substantiated that children born and raised in stable, loving, single parent families are doing just as well academically and behaviorally as their counterparts who are raised in two parent households.

Single Parents Provide Stability &
Overcompensate for the Absent Parent

Stability is important, coupled with the fact that children growing up in homes where single mothers have adequate economic and other social resources most likely will thrive and fare well because the parent is more involved. They are devoted to the success of their children and tend to overcompensate for the absence of the other parent in their child's life.

I must say, as a single parent, that I am guilty of this myself, overcompensating for the absent parent. This characteristic is prominent with most single parents that I have met and interviewed. Overcompensation is a survival skill and is also stemmed from the guilt we feel as single parents for the other parent not being there.

It is a heavy burden to bear, trying to compensate for a parent that is not present in your child's life, but it is instinctual as a single parent, trying to survive and help your children thrive with the cards dealt. However, it is rather gratifying to see that this instinctive, protective survival method is a positive that contributes to the success of the child.

I validate results of recent research from my own life experiences that stability is crucial and helps to determine the quality of life for children and adults. Children who feel safe and loved and feel a sense of security within themselves and within their family have the best opportunity to thrive. Children want to feel safe, loved and cared for. Adults, too, want to feel safe, loved and cared for. Having more financial resources does definitely help with security and knowing that you are not going to be evicted, but having a secure place to call home is comforting for children, their psyche and sense of well-being, as well as that of the parent.

So, when it is inevitable and you find yourself in a solo-parenting position, what do you do? How do you do it successfully and roll with the hand you have been dealt in the best way possible? How do you beat the odds and the negative stereotypes that are attached to single parents and their children? Do you become a statistic or do you defy them? The choice is yours, and yes, it is a choice. Yes, you would have preferred to be married, or have your spouse or child's father or mother in your life. This is the preferred situation, but it is not yours at the moment and it is out of your control at this time. You cannot roll back the clock or hit replay and start over. The reality is you are now a single parent and you have to learn to deal with it positively and get it right. You are not powerless; you can and *must* create the kind of life you want for yourself and your child/children.

We can reverse the undesirable stigma of single parents and children of single parents by being successful at solo parenting, by being SINGLE PARENTS THAT ROCK! We can have children who are successful by having higher expectations of our children and ourselves. We as single parents get to decide the quality of our lives and our children's lives. We don't have to let society and its negativity determines the quality and standards that we live up to. Let your life as a single parent, and how you raise your children, magnify the fact that "SINGLE PARENTS ROCK!"

(SECRET #2) MAY THE REAL SINGLE PARENTS STAND UP!

Do you know women who are married and say they feel like a single mom? Do you ever wonder what defines being a true single mom or dad? Not everyone may know what being a single parent really means. Some may say they feel like they are a single parent, but they really aren't. You are a single or solo parent if you live *alone* with the children and are solely responsible for their care. The other parent is not present in the home.

You can become a single parent in countless ways. It can be from separation or divorce. It can be from the death of one of the parents. It can be because a parent has to work and live away from the family or is in the military and it may be a temporary single parent situation. Single parenting can arise by choice of the parents. For instance, if they made a decision not to be together after the child is born, or they were never married, or maybe there was abuse in the home. A person can become a single parent by choosing to have a child independent of marriage, as a single parent adoption, in-vitro fertilization, surrogacy or one parent just not wanting to be involved and agreeing to be a sperm donor. As you can see, there are many ways single parent households come into existence, with some being by choice and others not by choice, such as in death or other traumatic circumstances.

> *No one knows what it is like to be a single parent unless they are one...*

As a single parent you have to deal with EVERYTHING ALONE. You are most often the only parent and/or the only one supporting your child. I was watching the Today show one morning and there was a segment about married women starting to "feel like a single mom." This immediately got my attention, and not in a good way. *How do married women know what it "feels like" to be a single mom? HELLO! The key word "married" is the telltale sign that you're far from being a SINGLE parent!* How dare these stay-at-home mothers attempt to compare their circumstances to that of a *single* mother simply because their husband comes home from work late and does not do his share of the housework or is traveling for his job to provide for the family? SERIOUSLY? As an actual single mom, this was insulting to me and very insensitive.

No one knows what it feels like to be a single parent unless they are or have been one, or if they are married and their spouse is away in the military—then they are justified in saying "I feel like a single parent" and really feel the strain of "being a single parent" because they actually *are* at the time, albeit with a great support system-the military helps take care of their own (and I love that!).

If your spouse is deployed, you are a solo parent doing it all alone, even if temporarily while your spouse is deployed or out of your home state for many months or even years. Your situation is like that of a single parent in many ways, although technically it's still not the same because you have someone who is longing to be with you and the children, and you may even have support for the family financially with deposits into a joint account. But you do have a more legitimate reason to really feel like a single parent. Your husband or wife is not just sacrificing for the family and not just away for short business trips; he or she is sacrificing for the entire country and is away for extended periods of time, and that is a huge difference.

People can try to empathize with single parents or

think they feel like a single parent, but the truth is, any situation where there is a spouse occupying the same home, assisting with chores and/or repairs, helping out in any way with the kids, bringing home a paycheck (or part of their paycheck), and present in their kids' lives in some capacity (although not as much as you or the children would like or need), that is not a single parent household. As difficult as it may be for you, it's so much harder for single parents!

Now that I have that off my chest, let me also say that any time you are a single mother raising your children and have great support from the father—either physically spending time with the kids or helping to support them financially—then you are in a great single parent position and should be extremely grateful. Most single parents do not have this type of support from the other parent. They are the truest form of single parents raising children alone and this is the most demanding situation you can be in.

If you are married or single with support from the other parent in any way, you have "support." If you have the child's other parent involved helping with major decisions regarding the kids, you are not truly alone and that is awesome. You have someone who can give you a break and share the responsibilities of decision-making, which allows the other parent to take a load off. You have someone who has a vested interest in raising your child to be the best they can possibly be without you having to be totally responsible for the good, bad or not-so-great decisions. This goes especially for when your children get older, because the decisions you are required to make become more difficult and can even be life altering. Even if you have financial support, this takes some of the burden off your shoulders—one less thing to worry about. You don't need to think about taking a first, second or third job, and therefore, more time away from your kids.

So, married women, I don't mean to be harsh, but you do have some assistance. Your husband may be traveling for work frequently and unavailable, leaving you alone to care for the children. I get it, you are stressed and would like more support. From a single mother's perspective, I would say be grateful that it is only temporary because you have no idea what it is like to be a true single parent in every sense of the word until you are doing it all and all of the time. I mean *everything* and doing it all ALONE. A so-called "do nothing husband" (as stated by some married women) or a husband whose job requires frequent travel or long hours away from home, does not compare to a truly "absentee father." You experience a snippet of what we go through as single parents, but it still does not compare.

There are things you can do to improve your situation. Communicate with your husband about the stress you are experiencing. Tell your husband what you need and what you expect from him in your partnership and how much it will take the load off your shoulders and ease some of your stress. Demand help from your spouse. If they are unwilling or unable to help as much as you need, then hire a housekeeper or nanny if you can afford it. Find ways to negotiate with your spouse to get them to do more, but appreciate what you do have—especially if the relationship/marriage is great.

I was having lunch with some co-workers of mine and one of the ladies shared some complications she was having with her teenage son immersing into pornographic sites on the internet. I really empathized with her situation, thinking to myself, *Wow, that is a tough one, how would I handle that?* It was challenging to say the least. As she continued telling her story, she said, "My husband and I discussed it and decided we would handle the situation in this manner…" I thought to myself, *She does not realize how wonderful it is to have someone help her manage this problem and decide together the most appropriate manner to handle it.* It was a delicate situation and a major life altering decision. Depending on how they responded, it could affect their relationship with her son, how he felt about himself, etc. She had someone else involved to figure it out, whereas with a single parent doing it alone, it's just you, and you just have to do it and pray you make the best decision…because it all falls on you if you don't.

(SECRET #3) SINGLE PARENTS ARE SUPERHEROES!

I am a single mother of a beautiful daughter who is now, as I begin writing this book, 18 years old. I am totally alone and have been since before I was legally divorced in December of 1999. My husband did not "die" after we were divorced, but you would think so because he has not been a part of my daughter's life since she was about five years old. He just decided that he did not have to be a father at all since we were no longer married and unable to work out the problems in our relationship. According to him, I was strong and independent and could do it all and so he just disappeared and went on with his life. I later heard the stereotypical phrases that you usually hear from "absentee fathers" like: *it's her mom's fault*; *she would not let me see my kid/kids*; *I don't want to give her any money because she will probably spend it on herself or her new man*; *I did not have a father figure in my life so I don't know how to be a father to someone else*; the list goes on.

It's all a bunch of CRAP! Just excuses and an unproductive blame game, point blank. Don't fall for the excuses and scapegoating which unfortunately a lot of people do, especially people on the outside looking in. Not being involved in a child's life that you helped produce shows poor character, lack of responsibility, no accountability, lack of respect and no love for yourself or your child. No one could ever in a million years keep me from being involved, present and active in my child's life. I would have to either be imprisoned or dead because I would fight like there is no tomorrow with everything I have for a quality, significant presence in my child's life. *No one* could keep me away!

I must awkwardly admit that I considered telling my daughter that her father "died" so she would not feel "abandoned" and have "abandonment issues" that are usually associated with children with an absentee parent. I know what you are probably thinking; that is awful, and how could I think about doing such a thing? It was extreme, but sometimes when you don't know what to do and are trying to protect your children, you may feel that you have to choose extreme measures. Although I temporarily pondered the idea, I definitively chose not to, and I am grateful I didn't.

Don't get me wrong, I do not dislike men, (or my ex

for that matter) I just don't appreciate the excuses from absentee mothers *or* fathers. There is no excuse for being an absentee parent when you are still living and breathing. I have wondered, *what if I presented excuses and chose not to be an active and fully engaged parent, where would my daughter be?* It is not fair to the children who did not ask to be born; they deserve so much more than a bunch of excuses. They deserve to be taken care of, respected, loved and cherished, and for someone to be there for them no matter what!

I know sometimes people are sick and struggling with drugs or alcohol abuse or maybe they are even mentally disturbed. In these instances it is best that they are out of their child's life, at least temporarily until they get it together. No one is perfect! But it does not mean they should be taking it easy or use this as an excuse to never be present eventually. They should be doing the work, whatever it takes, working on getting better so they can be fully existent as soon as possible, providing in every way possible for their children and being an active participant in their lives in a healthy manner.

Single Moms Are Extraordinary!

Many people don't realize what it is truly like raising children as a single/solo parent. Gloria Gaynor created the song "I Will Survive" and it is a single parent's anthem. Only the strong, determined, resilient, and focused will survive single parenting and get it right. They are true Single Parent Superheroes! Being a single parent is a full-time job all of the time—cooking, cleaning, shopping, fixing and repairing things that are broken in and outside of the house, doing yard work, laundry, homework, feeling guilty because your kids have to be in daycare all day, getting the kids to school, extracurricular activities, classes, rehearsals, sporting events, tutoring, meeting with teachers, open houses, and the list goes on and on. Not to mention working an *actual* full-time job outside of your home; sometimes two or three! You don't get a break. You barely get to do things for yourself. As single parents, we are truly extraordinary people. We are superheroes!

Raising kids alone is emotionally, physically and mentally draining, but so passionately rewarding, especially if you stay involved and focus on getting it right. You are doing *everything* alone. You are responsible for the finances and bringing home enough money to take care of the family alone. There is no second paycheck (unless you have a second job or side business); there is no child support (unless there is a mature, involved, responsible, non-custodial parent); there is no government assistance (unless you are in poverty); no financial aid for college especially if you are a middle-class, single, hardworking parent and are above the extremely low poverty line.

What Does a Single Parent Do?

You are responsible for making *ALL* of the decisions regarding parenting the kids: discipline, household duties, where you will live, how you will live, managing the household and finances, maintenance of the house inside and out including lawn care, painting, managing and repairing the car, handling disputes with teachers, their peers, helping with homework, knowing when to get a tutor and paying for one, first dates, first heartbreaks, explaining puberty and sex, birthday parties, graduation parties, preparing for SATs and ACTs, selecting the best courses and prep classes, college entrance applications and paying for all of these, helping to select the best university or college to attend and paying for it, graduation, prom, teaching them to drive, purchasing the best and safest car that you can afford, dealing with accidents—especially almost fatal accidents and the emotional anguish associated with it, keeping the kids healthy, eating properly, physical accidents and illnesses such as broken bones, chicken pox, upset stomachs, ear infections, cuts, bruises, sports accidents, doctors' appointments for everyone, cooking, cleaning, transportation of kids to different events, participating and showing up at the events they are involved in, feeling so guilty if you cannot, shopping for groceries, clothes, personal items, helping them establish friends and learn how to be a good friend, having play-dates with friends to build relationships, building relationships with the parents, teachers and others involved in their lives, going through their emotional growing pains in life with friends, disappointment and the many ups and downs of growing up, helping them learn to make decisions through each phase of their life that progressively gets more challenging for all involved, handling disappointments, heartaches and hurts...and on and on! You may even deal with your own feelings of isolation, loneliness, being the only single parent at the school event, athletic games or in church where there are basically only married couples in attendance, or your child feeling uncomfortable or not wanting to participate in traditional events such as a debutante ball because she is the only one who does not have a father to participate in the formal activities, etc. This list is exhausting and it does not cover the half of it.

My point is that when you are a single parent in America or anywhere, you do it all and it is no easy walk in the park. You feel all of the pains and heartaches that your children experience alone and it is more than anyone from a two parent household will fully understand or feel unless their situation changes and they experience it firsthand. There are no handouts or government assistance for single working moms, especially to the extent that some political parties and women-haters may suggest. You have to be in poverty to receive any assistance, and contrary to popular belief, not all single moms are in poverty.

Another Myth: Public Assistance

Unbeknownst to many is the fact that if you are a single parent of one child or maybe two you are not eligible for public assistance when you are working unless you are in poverty. You become eligible when you have multiple children and have an extremely low or no income and are considered impoverished. So if people are not making enough to make ends meet, pay for childcare, unable to purchase or afford health insurance, have a roof over their heads and feed their children, what are their options?

The design of the system creates the mentality of having more government assistance and support by having more children. It's no wonder why people have capitalized on this opportunity. I am never an advocate for having more children to get more government assistance, which should never be an option or a goal. My point is that if you are a working single parent who is being responsible and taking care of your children, you are not receiving government assistance, as people seem to suggest is the norm for all single parents.

The Facts about Public Assistance

The reality is that there are *not* a lot of resources available in the United States to positively support single parent families that are doing the best they can as compared to other countries. It has been reported that the U.S. does a lot less than its peer higher-income countries to assist and support efforts of success for single parent families as far as basic economic security, balancing work and family and having childcare assistance made available.

American single parents have the highest poverty rate, the lowest rate of health care coverage, the stingiest income support system, and also lack the paid time-off-from-work entitlements that other countries do to make it easier for single parents to balance caregiving and work. Americans must wait longer than single parents in comparison with other countries for early childhood education to begin and our government is always threatening to end it. When you research it, you find out so much more than what is usually broadcasted to keep the negativity hype up about single parents.

Balancing work and childcare is always a struggle, but

even more so with single moms. There is no support, and not much empathy or concern for assisting solo parents from the workplace. The mentality is every man or woman for himself, although most times it is the woman dealing with this issue and having to work outside of the home to support her family. When you do find quality childcare, it is not affordable and often more expensive to work and pay for childcare than it is to stay at home with your children. This is a choice that even two parent households have to make, but at least they can afford to make that choice.

Some politicians have suggested that we should discontinue the Head of Household exemption with IRS taxes so as not to reward people for having single parent households and encourage them to get and stay married…really? Our country wants to stigmatize single parent families instead of support them as they do two parent families? I am not asking for differential treatment, just equal treatment for all family household types. Depriving single parent families and punishing them does nothing to strengthen our community, our economy, our country or the welfare of our children and their future, nor yours. We must do better for the benefit of our shared communities and our shared country.

Single parents are not bad people; we are struggling, trying to take care of our families just like any man or woman in a two parent family. Children of single parents are not bad people, either. They are just humans in challenging circumstances. The real truth is that we are extraordinary beyond comparison. We are courageous, strong, resilient people, and a force to be reckoned with. Single parents are truly superheroes!

(SECRET #4) SINGLE PARENTS ARE STRONG AND COURAGEOUS!

As we grow into adulthood, most people hope to fall in love and get married to the man or woman of their dreams and eventually start a family. It is a simple dream: you meet someone you are attracted to, start dating, fall madly in love, become engaged, get married and make plans for spending the rest of your lives together. You have kids, the dog, house, white picket fence, and you grow your family. Children even have this dream and act it out in their imagination when they are little. It is embedded in us at an early age. Your thought pattern does not typically or initially consider the possibility of your marriage failing or even the possibility that you would be a single parent. You hopefully enter into marriage thinking and believing it will be "until death do us part." You are excited about the promises of the future for you and your family and the multitude of exciting life adventures and experiences waiting for you to explore, especially if you are a product of parents who stayed together. You are busy planning your future and life with your spouse and kids and all you can accomplish together as a team: two people united and ready to conquer the world together. Then *WHAM!* Out of nowhere something happens that changes everything, something that was not planned and something you never expected or dreamed would ever happen to you. You are now forced to deal with life and its changes.

My parents were married for 33 years until my father passed away after a three and half year fight with lung cancer, and although my ex-husband's parents were never married he still had the same hopes and dreams of having a lasting and fulfilling marriage. I always believed my marriage would last forever and we would have a couple of kids, a dog and the white picket fence, and our lives would be full of bliss. I never dreamed I would be divorced within seven years.

It Takes Bravery to Walk Away from Abuse and Venture into Single Parenthood

What most critics of single parent households—and single mothers especially—fail to understand is that it takes a lot for a woman or man who has been abused in any manner and continuously faced with living and trying to survive in an abusive and consistently destructive relationship to walk away. It takes a lot of courage, bravery, tenacity, and emotional and mental anguish to make the decision to leave, to separate your family in an effort to save yourself and your children from a lifestyle of hurt, pain and abuse. Furthermore, no one would intentionally select a mate, spouse or partner to marry, have children with and share their life with, knowing and expecting that they were doomed for a life of abuse and torture.

Staying in an abusive relationship and having your children witness abuse in any form on a consistent basis can be even more harmful to them indirectly and damaging to their healthy mental and emotional growth and development than living in a single parent home. It can also be harmful to children directly when they are recipients of the abuse. When abuse is in the household in any form, it does not discriminate as to which family members become the eventual targets over time. Being in an abusive marriage can undoubtedly be more destructive to the success of the children than living in a single parent household.

When researching for the writing of this book, I embarked on some interesting yet troubling opinions from critics about single parents on various forums. I read comments like: "The government and their entitlement programs is what is encouraging this behavior," or "do you think homosexuality is up because the father is not in the home?" Another accusatory comment on a forum was: "How dare these people be so inconsiderate and say *'oops it was an accident, I did not mean to get pregnant'*, when they did it on purpose."

It is rude, disheartening and offensive when you read and hear all of the negative, judgmental comments people make when they have no clue how we wind up being single parents, or the bravery it takes to venture out and make it on your own in an effort to save yourself and your children. No situation is the same; there are so many reasons people resort to or are circumstanced to being single parents. It can happen to just about anyone, as I mentioned earlier, so before people throw stones they need to remember that there are no vaccination shots to prevent single parenthood, so don't be surprised when single parent status knocks on your door with luggage and is ready to move in.

MY JOURNEY TO SINGLE PARENTHOOD
"Not a Destination but a Journey"

The story of my adventure as a single parent begins shortly after the birth of my one and only daughter in 1993. My baby girl developed jaundice (yellowing of the skin and eyes) within two weeks of her birth due to having an increased Bilirubin level in her blood. She had to be wrapped in a cocoon-type blanket device with special lights, called a Wallababy, most of the day for about a week or two. This was not ideal, but acceptable because I knew she would be getting better soon; I was a Pediatric RN (registered nurse) at the time and had to do this treatment in the hospital with other babies numerous times throughout my career.

I was living in Houston, Texas. My mom was visiting from Chicago and she and my husband got into a verbal disagreement over something very minor (whether I should eat before or after I took my walk outside for exercise… I already knew what choice I wanted for myself). It blew out of proportion quickly and I later realized it was more about who exerted the most control over me and each of them wanting to be right and more powerful than the other; it had nothing to do with what I wanted at the time.

My husband went to work that night as he had done every other night, but this time he did not come back in the morning, nor that afternoon or evening, not even for two or three days later, with no phone call or other contact whatsoever. I was devastated, stunned and scared out of my mind because this was unusual and had never happened previously.

It was also embarrassing as hell because my mother was in town and I had no clue what was going on. I thought maybe something happened to him; maybe he got sick, in a car crash or the unthinkable—possibly somewhere injured or dead. I called hospitals, police stations, family members, friends, co-workers and his job. I was all over the place mentally, and after many phone calls, I started to consider that maybe he was having an affair.

I called his mother in Flint, Michigan (she told me nothing, she never liked me and was probably gloating in my misery) and finally after many, many calls to his family locally, his aunt finally said, "Baby...I am sure he is all right and he will be home soon. You need to sit him down and talk to him and you will find out more about what is going on." This was extremely confusing to me. What did she mean by this? What the heck was going on?

By the time my husband returned home I was scared, angry, fuming, baffled and embarrassed. I had so many mixed emotions, and on top of it, weary from crying and dealing with my sick newborn. He looked tired, worn-out, his eyes bulging, had noticeably lost a few pounds in 48-72 hours, and looked just pitiful, nothing like the man who left for work days earlier. I had never witnessed him looking like this before. I was upset and amazed and could not stop spewing questions at him.

He then proceeded to tell me there was something I needed to know, that he was a "recovering drug addict" (I was stunned; this was all new to me) and began telling me about his drug addiction and how he had been in recovery for many years before we met but did not want to tell me because he thought he was OK and there was no need. He, of course, at the time blamed the argument he had with my mom as being what "triggered" him, then while he was en route to work he detoured off an exit to the Drug House. I was devastated. It did not seem real. I honestly felt that this must be a dream. How did I not know this? If the show "Punked" were out back then, I would have honestly felt that I was on it.

This was so overwhelming and way out of my life experiences and my comfort zone that I just could not relate. It was as if I was hallucinating. It was so surreal. How could I have chosen to marry a man who was a drug addict and I did not know it? I am an intelligent, educated, law abiding citizen, with good judgment and common sense. How could I have been attracted to someone with this problem? Those were the big questions. I was not judging him, but myself; it was more about the fact that I knew I deserved better than this and could not believe I made such a huge mistake and was not more vigilant in finding out more about the person I married and chose to have a child with.

Yes, it was all about me at the time because I was hurting, confused, unknowingly already going through post-partum depression and taking care of my sick newborn. I struggled with my choice in a mate and was devastated because I had no clue how to deal with such a challenging situation. I was just glad my mom was in town with me because although he blamed it on their argument, it was something he later admitted would have happened sooner or later anyway because he was not fully in recovery and had been increasingly drinking.

As I began to digest this new information over time, I realized I had noticed some peculiar behavior exhibited from him in the recent past that I could not figure out what it meant but was now beginning to make sense of. I noticed towards the end of my pregnancy that he started drinking more heavily and I discussed this with him, thinking about alcoholism, but never would I have thought that he was a recovering drug addict. I later realized that when I met him he was not in recovery because I met him at a nightclub. He introduced himself while offering to buy my girlfriend and I a cocktail along with his. If you are in recovery, you are definitely not drinking!

I initially decided to stay and support him because he swore that it would not happen again and he would get back on track and go to meetings. I was naïve and wanted to believe him until a few days later when he stayed out again, not returning home for a few days. This time my immediate response was to get the hell out of dodge. I was terrified, confused and did not know what I had gotten myself into or what to expect. I heard tragic stories regarding drug addicts being high out of their minds and mistaking their family members and loved ones for evil spirits/demons and seriously injuring or even killing them in a rage of self-defense. I had a close girlfriend and my mother both pleading in each ear with me to leave because they were also fearful for my well-being. My mother was afraid and was ready to flee and I did not want to be left alone to deal with this massive beast of a problem. I decided I could not handle all of this and a sick baby, so I packed up my little black car, my mom and newborn, and left home on a 17-hour drive back to Chicago out of fear of the unknown. This was not what I had signed up for. I was fearful and worried because I didn't have much knowledge about drug addiction but had heard plenty of horror stories.

While back in my hometown of Chicago, I went through weeks of soul searching. I was lost; this was foreign territory to me. It was a lot to deal with all at one time and looking back, I must say that I am proud of how I was able to get through it and how strong I was to handle it all without completely breaking down and losing my mind. I realize now that I was never alone. God was with me the whole time.

After being away for nearly two months—with lots

of crying, praying, weight loss, and nurturing my soul and my daughter—I eventually made the decision that I needed to go back. This was despite protests from my family; they also had fears of the unknown path that I was journeying and being a 17-hour drive away from them. I knew I initially left Houston and ran out of panic and fear because I honestly had no idea what to do. I needed time to think and get myself together, but I also knew I could not just quit and leave without attempting to help him and save our marriage. I had taken an oath and promise to God and my husband to love each other in sickness and in health…and he was definitely sick. I felt I needed to be loyal to him, our marriage and to our daughter and I had to at least make a concerted effort. I told myself, "If the tables had been reversed and it was I going through this, I would want him to at least try to help me." I owed this to me as well so that I would not have any regrets later thinking I should have or could have done something different. I had to live with myself and my decisions, and no one else.

He came to pick my daughter and me up after being away a couple of months and we made the 17-hour drive back to Houston. I was undeniably nervous and going to face the unknown but I researched and attended a few Al-Anon (Alcoholics Anonymous) and Nar-Anon (Narcotics Anonymous) meetings and knew God was with us so I felt more equipped. I had resources and I knew where to find support.

I tried with everything in me to stick in there 'till death do us part' and help him with his addiction, but I was the one doing more of the helping. He was not helping himself. I attended Al-Anon and Nar-Anon meetings weekly and sometimes several times a week. I started receiving counseling and even tried marriage counseling with a minister at our church. Whatever I could do, I tried to offer support and learn more about what we were dealing with. I truly loved him and desperately wanted to keep our family together, and I believed it was possible.

My life was going in a downward spiral. The more I tried to help, the lower I was pulled into this spiraling HOLE, physically, mentally, emotionally, spiritually, financially, and it was not good for myself or our daughter. I was losing weight and even had to stop breastfeeding after only three months because I was not producing enough milk. I later discovered I was going through postpartum depression and just did not know it at the time. It was challenging and sometimes scary because I never knew what to expect and if the sober or cracked-up version of my husband would walk in the door, but I consider myself a strong person and that is what kept me sane—that and my spirituality and seeking out as much help as possible.

The home life became so unbearable for me that I began to not feel safe in my own home especially with him standing over me in the dark as someone other than my loving husband, fiercely threatening and demanding the keys to my car (because he had sold his for drugs). I would not wish this disease on anyone, especially the family that has to deal with the sporadic and unpredictable behavior. I separated a few times from my husband, even moving back to my hometown of Chicago, ultimately for good when I became fearful for myself and my daughter's life and emotional stability. After many failed reconciliation attempts, I finally separated for the very last time in 1996 when my daughter was three years old. I was legally divorced in December of 1999 when she was six, which was also around the last time she saw him. I made the decision that I was not going into the millennium still legally married, although we were no longer together. By this time I felt I had done everything I could do. This was something he had to tackle on his own when he was ready. I knew I could now leave without any regrets and I truly did "Let Go and Let God".

New Beginnings as a Single Mom Doing it Alone

After much anguish, emotional and mental distress, I had to make the decision to part ways and file for a divorce. I went to Markham County Courthouse in Illinois and asked for the appropriate papers, filled them out, paid the required fee, filed for my divorce and showed up on the assigned court date. It was time for new beginnings. Now it was just Mini-Me and I. Just the two of us. I was now officially a divorced, single parent. Because my husband was not present and I could not locate him at the time of my divorce, he was never issued a child support order. As a result of this and his non-attempts of being involved, he has never supported her in any way physically, emotionally, mentally, nor financially since she was four or five years of age, before we were officially divorced. He has continued to battle his addiction for many years.

No matter what your journey is to single parenthood, once you get there most people will have the same thoughts and fears. How can I do this alone? How are we going to make it? What do I do now? It is scary and confusing, and no one who arrives at this junction automatically knows what to do. We all want to excel and be the best parent possible but we just don't know how or where to start sometimes.

I was like many of you: scared, confused, angry, disappointed. I felt betrayed by life because my dreams of my life and happy journey with my family intact were shattered. I never conceived that I would be parenting all alone, and being everything to my daughter as I worked a full-time job trying to support my household. I was still growing up myself, trying to do it all and survive. I was terrified. I learned that dealing with the other major issues (the loss of a marriage, life partner or relationship, and the failure of it all in general) can be downright depressing along with trying to survive as a single parent.

I had to get it together because my daughter was depending on me. *You* have to get it together because your kids are depending on you! I searched high and low for books or other resources to help me learn to be the best single parent I could be and I could not find anything. This was twenty years ago. I did find several books on parenting that were extremely beneficial with foundational topics, but nothing on dealing with issues from the perspective of a single mom or single parent family. I had to improvise and do the best I could. This is one of the reasons I wanted to write this book, so I could share my experiences in order to help someone else living in the trenches of the single parent life.

(SECRET #5) SACRIFICES ARE DOUBLY ESSENTIAL FOR SINGLE PARENTS

Do you ever wonder about the success and quality of your child's life being from a single parent household? Many of us do. I know I still wonder, because the truth is revealed with who they become in the future. I am a firm believer that quality, consistent, active parenting is what determines the excellence and quality of life that your children inherit. This type of parenting is not easy; it requires a lot of work and sacrifice but can be so rewarding for both you and your child/children. It involves being consistently present in your child's life with unconditional love, listening to them, allowing them to speak, asking questions, constantly teaching them morals, and helping them learn from the consequences of their actions. Active parenting also involves instilling core values and beliefs, developing rituals, habits and high expectations, promoting age-appropriate independence, and being mature enough to make certain sacrifices in your own life (now this is really huge).

Making sacrifices as a parent is extremely important. Because of your single parent status, these sacrifices double and there is no getting around it. There is only one of you and you are doing the job of two, so something has to give when you are putting your children's needs and priorities before yours. It is something you'll find you have to do more times than not. This is where some people mess up in both solo parent and two parent households.

Sometimes parents can be too selfish and are unwilling to make sacrifices for their children, especially at the most crucial times. Part of this may be because they are still young and immature and not wanting to sacrifice for the sake of the children. Being a parent, and especially a single parent, there is no getting around it. You have to adjust your attitude and realize that it is no longer just about you. You have to grow up and put on your big girl panties or big boy boxers.

I appreciate single or married people who realize they are too selfish to have children and thus make the decision to never have children for this and other reasons. It is very mature and responsible because when you have children you have to make many sacrifices; letting go of selfishness is one of them. This should not be a chore. If you don't want to make sacrifices, don't have children.

What Types of Sacrifice Are Necessary?

Sacrificing your time and being available is especially important for disciplining your children, which we will discuss in greater detail later. You have to be present to enforce rules as well as punishments, and be there with them when your children are grounded. You have to sacrifice your partying and your outings with friends at times to be present in your children's lives. You have to sacrifice having as much time alone or uninterrupted; you can't just do whatever you want when you want to do it. You might even have to sacrifice where you live, what type of housing or neighborhood you live in, or who you live with. Your living situation may have been fine when you were single without children or even if you were married, but it may not be conducive to the safety and health environment for your children.

Sacrifice may also involve being away from your children to pursue education, job opportunities, or working more than you'd like in order to make ends meet. You may have to sacrifice romantic relationships for a while or going out on dates as much, which we will also discuss later. You may have to sacrifice certain relationships and friendships that don't vibe well with your single parent life and the safety and security of your children.

Many times, you have to sacrifice spending money on new clothes, a new car or getting your hair and nails done in order to pay bills or so that your children can go on field trips and participate in school or sports-related activities. You have to sacrifice your time and energy to attend these school-related or extracurricular activities. You may also have to sacrifice sleep sometimes to get it all done. The list goes on and on. As you can see, making sacrifices is a fact of life for single parents.

Sacrifice is a Responsibility and Takes Maturity and Commitment

It takes a lot of growth, maturity, responsibility and love to make sacrifices. Single parents have to be strong. It also takes strength and commitment to make sacrifices and be available as a parent. It is unfortunate that sometimes both parents, whether together or not, do not make these sacrifices for the sake of the children. Often it is just the mother making the majority or all of the sacrifices. Most often, our society condemns single mothers for not having a man present in their lives. Women get the brunt of the criticism for the failure of the two parent family. Society may blame fathers for being the stereotypical "dead beat dad" and not fulfilling their financial duties of supporting the children that they have helped to conceive, but until just recently, you would hardly hear reference to the importance of the father's presence in their child's life and the impact it has when they are absent.

Unfortunately, with children raised in single parent households, it is always one parent being present, accounted for and responsible. Most times, but not always, it is the mother that is making all of the sacrifices for the sake of the children while it is easier for fathers to walk away and not fulfill their economic or other fatherly responsibilities to make sure their children are fed, clothed, loved, secure and properly cared for. This is not the case in all single parent families. There are increasing numbers of households where the father has stepped up as the solo parent and is doing it alone, being responsible and making sacrifices. In these situations, the mother has decided to walk away without supporting the children financially, being present or sharing in her motherly responsibilities. In fact, statistics show that 16% of custodial single parents are men, which is about 1.96 million single fathers as of 2012 (census.gov 2012 data). So the pendulum can swing both ways. The key is that sacrifice is crucial in parenting, and doubly so for single parents.

You don't have to be wealthy to be successful at parenting. We all know that wealthy, famous kids can also turn out horrid, even in two parent households. If you don't have an abundance of money or financial resources, you can still provide a quality of life that promotes and encourages your children to grow up as happy, healthy, law abiding, intelligent, successful, thriving citizens with strong ethical character because there are so many resources available to help you with your journey. The biggest resource available is YOU and it all starts with having the right mindset to be responsible, committed, consistent, and to make the important sacrifices by any means necessary!

Remember, our children should not have to sacrifice so that we can have the lives we deserve (as the parents), but we as the parents should make sacrifices so our children can experience the lives *they deserve*!

(SECRET #6) GOD LOVES SINGLE PARENTS AND THEIR CHILDREN

Do you ever feel totally alone and isolated raising a child as a solo parent? Do you wonder if God is with you and your family and hears your prayers? You are not alone in feeling this way; it is challenging not to at times. My little girl was a good baby, if I may say so myself. God knew that I would be alone most of the time as a single parent and He blessed me with a wonderful baby girl. He has demonstrated time and time again that even when I felt alone, I was never truly alone; that He is with me always and has always showed up right on time making His presence known. There have been so many instances of this demonstration, but I will share with you some of the major life-changing moments where His presence was made known definitively.

I knew when my daughter was just about nine months old that she was special and God was taking care of us. After returning to Houston from Chicago for my first reconciliation attempt with my ex-husband, I was living alone with my daughter and became extremely ill. I was not sure at the time what was going on with me physically, just that my body was trying to fight off a horrific virus or some other illness. I remember having only enough energy to lay a blanket down on the floor after taking some medicine to help me feel better. I was physically, mentally and emotionally exhausted and I did not know how I was going to get through the day and take care of my nine-month-old daughter feeling as awful as I did. I literally could not move.

We both lay on a blanket on the floor and (by the grace of God) slept for at least 12 hours straight, waking up late at night. We had slept through the entire day and I felt 200% better; I could not believe she slept that long because it never happened before and surely did not happen anytime soon after that. God knew I was sick, totally exhausted mentally and physically, and that I could not handle any more at the time. He blessed me with what I needed to make it through that day and night as He has done many times before and after that. I am just more aware since that day. The Bible says that God does not give you more than you can handle and that night truly made me a deeper believer because I was fully aware that

I had experienced it firsthand.

God Will Take Care of You...

You are never truly alone. God does take care of you whether you know it or not and He shows up when you least expect it, which is always right on time. You may feel alone many times but trust me, you are not. God loves single parents, as well as our children, just as much as anyone else. He knows what we need when we may not know what we need ourselves. He is our significant other that we can depend on to be there for us.

Another instance in which God showed up spontaneously and definitively, which I will never forget, was when my daughter was three years old. I was separated at this time, had moved back to Chicago and was going through the normal stresses of single parenting and unknowingly experiencing lingering depression from a failed marriage. There are always things that go wrong in life, and boy was I having my fair share of it at this stage. I was emotionally depleted this one evening and suddenly my halogen light bulb blew out. I figured, OK, don't panic, no stress, just fix the problem. It was simple and I could handle it. I drove to Menards (my favorite home improvement store at the time) and purchased the replacement bulb. I returned home feeling like a productive problem solver. I struggled with the light to detach the screws, take out the old bulb, replace it with the new bulb and re-attach the screws. Mind you, I am not a handy woman so this was a real struggle, although I remained patient and felt I had accomplished a great feat when I got it done.

I was already upset and worried with so many other things on my mind. At this time, I was not the kind of person who would reach out for the help that was available from my parents and friends because I was so used to doing things on my own. I never wanted to "bother" anyone, so imagine the load I was carrying on my shoulders. Well to make a long story short, I plugged the halogen lamp back into the socket expecting it to turn on immediately and light up my life and it did not. I struggled and played with it some more and nothing happened. This was such a small thing in the scheme of life, but this small thing was "the straw that broke the camel's back" and started an avalanche of tears and emotions that were buried so deep inside of me. I sat there on the bed in the dark just bawling. Everything hit me at once like a ton of bricks so unexpectedly; I was definitely having a moment.

Surprisingly, in walks my three-year-old daughter from playing in the living room. I was surprised because there was no way she should have been able to hear me or know that I was crying. She was there physically, but what happened next blew me away and stopped my crying instantaneously. She walked over to me and placed her right hand on my back and starting rubbing my back as she spoke to me. I will never forget the words she said: "Don't cry, it's OK Mommy, everything is gonna be OK. God will take care of you. God loves you. He is taking care of us. It is OK to ask for help sometimes. You gotta ask for help, Mommy. You don't have to do it all by yourself, OK? People want to help you. All you have to do is ask and everything will be ok. OK?" She told me she loved me and then ran out of the room with her three-year-old body and commenced playing again with her toys in the living room like nothing ever happened.

I was totally flabbergasted and wondered, *what just happened?* I realized right away and was in awe at the fact that God had just spoken to me through my three-year-old daughter. She had just spoken to me as if she were an adult. I literally felt the presence of God's spirit connecting to me spiritually via my daughter, relaying a message of love, hope and encouragement. There was no other explanation. I received the message and knew without a doubt that God was speaking to me through her. He wanted me to know that: "You are strong and independent but it is OK to ask for help." This totally changed my life forever. It was the second big awareness that God was watching over us.

God Shows Up Right on Time... You Can Depend on HIM!

More recently, God has shown up in another big and fabulous way. I know He is always there and working His blessings in my life, but He did it again in such a BIG way when my daughter was seventeen years old, on prom night. She was driving her car from an after prom "lock-in" that ended at 5am. The night of her prom, my friends and I saw her off and we continued to drink champagne and wine until she and her escort left at about 1am. At about 4:30am I woke up suddenly and realized that my daughter was not home but should be home soon, and thought maybe I should go and pick them up from the event. I quickly decided against it because I had been drinking and only had about two hours of sleep. I felt it would not be responsible or a great idea, so I fell back asleep.

At about 5:30am I received the most horrifying call from my daughter. She was crying uncontrollably and trying to speak at the same time. I sat straight up, panicked, shaking hysterically, not knowing what was going on and unable to understand her. I pleaded with her to calm down some, communicate with me and help me understand, and she informed me that she had been in a car accident and that her car had flipped over and she was stuck in it. I jumped out of bed to my feet and started grabbing clothes to put on as quickly as possible, while I asked her to tell me where she was. She told me her location and that OnStar was sending the police and I was out of the house with my mother in tow (she happened to be in town for prom and graduation) all within three minutes or less. I fled to the scene, which was only about five minutes away from the house. I think I made it in two minutes but it seemed like forever. I remember my mom pleading with me to slow down because she was afraid we would get into an accident or drive off the two-lane road or something.

When we arrived I was hysterical, terrified and did not know what to expect. I was flooded with emotions and my adrenaline was pumping fast. I became elated and relieved but still shaking profusely when I made it to my daughter. There were other adults and teens that were coming from the lock-in who witnessed the accident and immediately tried to assist them. My daughter and her escort were out of the car, but she was shaking and crying while being consoled by another parent. Although my heart was beating extremely fast, I was so relieved when I saw her and hugged her ever so tightly, I could not calm down. She was walking; I did not see any physical injuries and all she kept saying was, "Mom, I am so sorry, I don't know what happened." I kept telling her, "It is OK, you are alive and safe and everything will be OK." Her prom escort was OK as well, although he acquired a couple of minor bruises near the right side of his rib cage. I was ecstatic and relieved that they both had survived this traumatic experience. The car was completely totaled and looking at it from the perspective of a passing observer or actual witness, one would have assumed there were no survivors; that is how damaged the car was, as if no one could have walked away from the accident.

GOD Saved My Daughter's Life!

"It was a *miracle* that they survived this crash," is exactly what the sheriff stated, who investigated the case and was at the scene. He informed me that if the car had hit the utility pole head-on they would not have survived, but it was the right wheel of the car that hit the pole and the car flipped over.

I knew without a doubt that it was nothing but almighty GOD who had saved my baby girl and her prom escort. Only He works miracles and that was definitely a miracle. I cried for days from the pain of thinking that I could have lost my daughter that night – on prom night before she graduated from high school. I also cried from unexplainable JOY of knowing that God was taking care of my daughter. It was basically like He was saying, "You don't have to worry. I've got this."

No matter how much I tried to protect my daughter from dangers, no matter how much worrying I did, it was impossible for me to be everywhere and to do everything to protect her, but God and His angels were. Of course, initially, I kept telling myself that I should have picked them up, that she was not used to driving after being up all night, that I should have worked the lock-in although they informed me they did not need more volunteers, and that I should have just gone anyway. All of the "should've" stuff that I could think of, you know, that thing we do as parents sometimes or for some of us, all of the time: we beat ourselves up after the fact as if we could have been all-powerful, all-knowing and prevented something from happening, or we fool ourselves into thinking we have this false sense of control and power.

Then I had to remember to be grateful again and accept the fact that I cannot be everywhere and that I cannot protect her from everything, but what I can do is continue to pray. I have always prayed for her. I have definitely been a praying momma. God heard me and was showing me that He was there and He was answering my prayers. He has been and will always be there for us. He also wanted me to know that I was powerless over the situation, as well as most other situations, but God is in control. That traumatic experience was a true lesson for me that forever changed the lives of me and my daughter.

I learned that I am not alone, my daughter is not alone, and God will take care of us. Don't get me wrong, I still worry sometimes because I am not perfect. I am a parent and that is what we do as parents, but I also know and truly believe that God and His angels are protecting my daughter and watching over her all of the time. This definitely lessens the worry and is extremely reassuring when I remember it.

There have been several instances throughout my solo parent family life where God has shown me that He is here with us, protecting us and guiding us. If you have a spiritual foundation, this can be extremely beneficial to tap into during the many challenges you will face as a single parent, especially when you are feeling alone. It is good to know that you are not.

The truth is that often as a single parent it feels like you are in it alone, but remember what God says in Isaiah 43:2-3: "When you pass through the waters, I will be with you. When you cross rivers, you will not drown. When you walk through fire, you will not be burned, nor will the flames hurt you. This is because I, the Lord, am your God, the Holy One of Israel, your Savior." He is always with us.

It is awesome to get those signs of encouragement to remind you that you are not alone, you are strong, have all that you need to survive, and that you can get through this and things will get better. Be still, pray and meditate daily. Find ways to get centered and tap into your inner spiritual energies to renew your spirit and feed your soul on a daily basis. If you get really quiet and pay close attention, you will realize you are not alone. God is with you and your family. He is taking care of you.

(SECRET #7) IT REALLY DOES TAKE A VILLAGE TO RAISE A CHILD

During a second separation from my ex (we had at least three before we divorced) when my daughter was young, I moved back home from Houston to Chicago to live permanently. My dad was sick and diagnosed with Stage 4 lung cancer and was given 6-9 months to live and I wanted to be there with him and my mom and allow my daughter time to get to know her grandparents, and especially her grandpa before he passed. This happened at a time when I was having problems anyway and knew my marriage was over.

Fortunately for us, my dad was a fighter and remained alive three and a half more years before he passed away. Moving back home to spend the quality and quantitative time with him was the best decision I made. My father became my daughter's surrogate dad and he truly loved spending time with her whenever he could and as much as possible. He fully engaged and played with her in ways that he never did with my siblings and I as we were growing up. I truly believe this experience was as therapeutic for him spiritually, mentally and physically as it was for my daughter, and it helped him continue to fight his disease and survive longer.

My father was blessed with an opportunity to truly be a grandfather before he passed away and he was extremely proud of this role and took it seriously. My daughter watched sports with him and knew all of the big-time wrestlers by name. He played grocery store and cash register with her until *she* got tired, not him. They celebrated and had a birthday party together when she turned four. It was such a wonderful relationship she experienced with him and it was truly a joy for me to watch.

Good Grandparents Are a Blessing!

Relationships with grandparents are extremely important and beneficial to both the children as well as the adults. If the grandparents are emotionally and mentally healthy and willing to be actively involved in your children's lives, it needs to happen. If there are problems of incest, child abuse, drug, alcohol abuse or violence with the grandparents or other family members living or present in the same home as grandparents, then by all means, definitely keep them far away from your children for their own physical, mental and emotional stability. This is a non-negotiable no-brainer.

Unfortunately my father passed away when my daughter was five years old after battling cancer for three and a half years. This caught the family by surprise because he had lived longer than predicted and had been doing well. My dad was here one day, happy healthy and active, and passed away twenty-four hours later due to complications with administering his chemotherapy and his development of sepsis. This was very traumatic and I was suddenly faced with such a dilemma, so many questions. How do we, as a family, cope with this? How do I help my mom and my other family members when I myself am grieving?

We were not prepared; we got comfortable again with him being with us for three years after initially being given six to nine months to live when he was initially diagnosed. I was also faced with the major decision of whether or not to allow my daughter to come to the hospital with the family when they called us back to the hospital for his final breaths to say our goodbyes, or if I should just send her off to stay with friends. I chose the latter and she spent the night with a friend of hers. I was glad I did at the time, because it was an extremely emotional event, lots of crying, as he was not aware of who we were and I did not know how she would react or if I could take care of her emotionally the way I would need to when I was trying to hold it together myself and take care of my mom at the same time. My daughter was young and did not understand it much.

That was one of the most difficult and life changing events in my life. Not only was I losing a parent, my father who had been with me my entire life, but she was losing the only other real father figure in her life. Little did I know at the time how critical that would be for her, because there were no other real men that could replace or substitute that void for her in the years to come.

How Do You Explain the Death of a Loved One to a Child?

This is how I handled informing her that her best friend and grandpa had passed away. The day after he passed away, we went to our favorite spot, a very small community park in Flossmoor, IL, to sit and talk. There was a little circular pond with ducks and we sat on our favorite swinging bench as we always did to talk, although this talk would be much different. This was the most difficult thing I needed to do; I had to explain to her that she would never see her "Poppa" again and that he had gone away to heaven. It was difficult for me because it was so sad and final; I was grieving and emotionally distraught, but also because I felt I would have a difficult time explaining the situation so that she could understand it at five years old.

I don't think she was able to really grasp at the time that he was not ever coming back because she kept asking, "So when he is gone to heaven will he not come and play with me anymore?" This was a difficult concept for her to accept and understand because her grandpa was her buddy, her friend, and her playmate. Her next and final time seeing him was at the funeral, lying in the casket. I struggled back and forth with whether or not it was a good idea to let her attend the funeral but I wanted her to have closure as best as she could at a young age. She handled it well and was still not fully aware of the finality of it all for a little while.

To this day, she does not even remember the funeral, so I guess it was OK and it did not scare her or freak her out. She still misses him and has fond memories of him and their special time together. I also make sure that I continue to talk about their special times to keep the memories alive as well as allow her to look at pictures and home movies when she says she is starting to forget. I don't want her to forget, because it was something special. Sure it brings sadness but it also brings pleasure and comfort to remember those times. It is so bittersweet.

Death of a close family member is something that we all have to deal with as adults. The real challenge comes when it happens while our children our smaller and we have to deal with their understanding and emotions as it relates to death. This is a very delicate but important component of growth and development for children. There are many books available that address this issue. I did not have the time to research it when I went through this with my daughter. You have to decide what is best for your child and most appropriate for their age and level of understanding. You must consider how you want to handle this personal and delicate life-changing situation.

I do want to stress that you should acknowledge

your children during the grieving process and allow them to express how they feel and how their situation will change because this other person will no longer be in their lives. Some kids may require counseling to help them learn to deal with the emotions they are feeling related to the loss, and they may not even understand these emotions themselves. Remember that they are grieving as well, although it might not be as obvious to you or even to them. They need the time and attention to get through the process of grieving and loss, just as you do.

Village Family Support

If you are blessed to have other family members around that you care about and they are healthy, allow your kids to spend time with them. If you are not comfortable with your kids having sleepover nights away, invite their kids over to spend time with you; the parents will appreciate you for it. Allow them to develop relationships with their cousins and other family members. This is important to their healthy growth and development and it also becomes important later when they want to know their family and feel the love and support of being part of a strong extended family unit.

My daughter grew up the lone child in our extended family. Her cousins were much older so there was no one in the family that had children near her age to develop close relationships with, so friends and schoolmates became her social circle. If at all possible, allow your children to get to know the absent parent's family as well so they can develop those relationships and know who their family is—*all* of their family. I believe it is the responsibility of the other parent to ensure this but when they don't show up and if you have a relationship with members of the other family, you can foster it with your children.

When our kids are born, most parents develop a strong caretaking response and will do anything to protect their kids. Naturally, when it is time to go to work after your kids are born, one of the greatest challenges is deciding whom to trust to take care of them. If you have parents, aunts or cousins that are close to you and are mentally and physically able and willing to help you out, then you are blessed. When you don't have this luxury, then there is a process that you must go through to find appropriate childcare that you are comfortable leaving your kids with. This can be challenging, but it is not impossible. You must begin with due diligence and start early, even before your child is born if possible, for your newborns and toddlers.

It really does take a village to raise a child! I have a very small immediate family. I have been grateful to have my mother still alive and she has been a blessing assisting with my daughter. It is wonderful watching their relationship develop and get stronger over the years. My sister was also extremely active and involved in my daughter's life while she was younger and has been a wonderful aunt for her over the years. There are additionally a few close friends that I have known for many years that have become surrogate aunts and uncles and have loved and cherished her as well. When you are a single parent, it is truly a blessing to have people in your life that care about you, and more importantly, that care about and support your child. They become your family and your children recognize them as family. If they have children, your children can grow up together and you can assist each other with childcare, etc.

When developing your village family, make sure you are teaching your children that families come in all different shapes, sizes and formations. While they are in school they most likely will see a two parent, heterosexual family common in their environment, depending on where they live, and begin to feel and see that their family situation is different. You want to assure them that although their family may look different, or is structured a little differently, yours is no less of a family unit than any other. It is just different, and there is nothing wrong with being different or unique. You also have to sometimes stress this to their teachers who might also not be accepting of the various types of family structures and will unintentionally make your child feel uncomfortable because of their differences.

Adopting a Community Village Family

If for some reason you don't have a strong extended family and friends, or you have moved somewhere new and unfamiliar, then adopt your church family or your neighbors and develop a strong community family. Allow your kids to participate in playgroups or develop them yourself with the help of friends and neighbors. This allows your kids to play and you can have some adult bonding time, as well. This way you will not feel alone and you can also support each other in other ways such as babysitting, sharing recipes, repairs, etc. Think of it as a great network for you and your kids, and you might even develop some lasting friendships and support systems.

When I moved, one of the best ways I met other parents was to pick up my daughter from school when she was young and begin to talk with the other parents that were also there standing and waiting to pick up their children, or while attending school functions or trips. You can also meet your neighbors by allowing your children to play outside. Children will naturally interact with one another. Walk your children to the bus stop if you are home, and wait with other parents, as they are doing the same thing. Begin introductions and conversations and eventually you will be walking back in the same direction towards home, talking and getting to know one another, and then maybe even having coffee together if time permits.

You will be quite surprised to discover how many other parents are just like you, whether married or a single, that need support and friendship with other parents. Some may have recently relocated and are new to the area just as you are and don't have family and friends or a support system in place. You will be amazed at how many people you will start to meet that have a lot in common with you and are excited to meet you as well. It takes a little bit from you, such as being available and open to forming new relationships.

Sometimes, as single parents, we get so used to doing it all alone that we unintentionally close ourselves off and put up towering walls around us and our children. So, it will take a little concerted effort in the beginning to open up a little and not be so independent or defensive.

Know the Village Family BEFORE Giving Them Access to Your Children

Take the time to really get to know these other parents. Before you can trust someone with your children, who are your prized possessions, you have to really get to know these other people, their family and what is going on in their household. This will allow you to slowly lower the walls you have built to protect yourself and your children. Trust is earned and is built over time—both for you and for them. You have to take the time and energy to learn their values, morals, standards, parenting styles, household status and environment to ensure that this friendship is viable and that this person is worthy of being a part of your support system and village. Likewise, you must be patient and allow them to trust you as well. If you or your children are uncomfortable in any way with them or others in the family, move on to the next... This is a process of elimination. This is the family that you get to choose, so choose wisely, because your children depend on your judgment and thorough investigation of the people you allow to be a part of their village.

Childcare

Having and developing relationships with other parents will allow you to have assistance with childcare. You can take turns keeping each other's kids or having them over for play dates or sleepovers when it's age appropriate. If your children are comfortable and really do like the parent and their children, this will be a fun treat for them as well. They may also have older children that can assist with childcare and offer babysitting services. Other parents are a great resource for referrals of cost-effective quality childcare. They may have relatives, know people in their church for hire, or know local college students that may be looking for work and can assist with after school and weekend.

Finding and maintaining appropriate, quality, safe childcare is a major issue with parenting in general, but especially with single parents. We have to be resourceful and utilize the relationships we have built with friends, family, neighbors and others in the community. The most difficult aspect that we face in utilizing and developing a village of support is just asking people for help. You will be amazed at how many people want to help and support you (especially if you have children that are well behaved for the most part) and they may even help for free or for a small fee. Seek out head-start programs, subsidized government childcare providers and resources, as well as company and work-related childcare.

For school-aged children, there are many after-school programs available for subsidized or low cost prices either at your child's school, the local YMCA, Boys & Girls Club in the area, local churches, etc. If there are local colleges or universities, there are definitely students who are looking for extra work and may provide babysitting services for your children after school and on the weekends. You can negotiate a reasonable and affordable rate that is appropriate for all involved. Be sure to perform your due diligence and, when possible, use referrals from other parents or people you trust.

Your neighbors, who you have developed relationships with, may also be willing to help you out and you can barter services in exchange for them helping with your children; maybe you can help with decorating, repairs, grocery shopping, etc. As single parents we have to get creative, reach out and find the available resources because they are out there. We have to be willing to give in order to receive, which includes giving up some of our conveniences, hesitancies, comfort levels, distorted perceptions, and also giving up our strong sense of INDEPENDENCE.

We all need other people in our lives. We cannot survive alone, no matter how tough or strong we are. It is also so much more fun and rewarding to share our lives and experiences with others in a healthy and nurturing way. It is OK to ask for help sometimes! We can all help each other in some way. Our village can become our family if we are open to receive it in a smart, loving and conscientious manner.

(SECRET #8) CREATE AND CHERISH MEMORIES WITH YOUR CHILDREN

How many times have you heard the statement "cherish the memories"? I'm sure you've heard it many times, but how many times—especially when you are young—do you really ponder and realize how important this statement is and what it means in your life? We, as parents, need to first make time to actively participate and create positive, enjoyable memories with our children, and then we need to hold onto and cherish those memories. It is not a cliché! Creating and cherishing memories helps build strong relationships and a sense of family and family legacy. When I say this, I am referring to happy, positive, fun, meaningful memories; not tragic, unhappy or painful memories. Try to make the good times outnumber the bad times. As the saying goes, "YOLO"—which means "you only live once"—and we never know how much time on this earth is promised or what will happen tomorrow.

I find myself intentionally and persistently doing

things to ensure that my daughter remembers the special times she shared with her grandpa by showing old videos that I made of them together, sharing pictures and talking about their shared experiences and how much he loved her. She still remembers some things even at 18 years old because we constantly replay and cherish the memories.

Various Ways to Create and Store Memories...

Over my adult and parenting years, I have learned to truly respect and appreciate the value of creating memories, knowing they can last a lifetime and are priceless. The longevity of memories depends on your individual effort of keeping them alive with your kids. Children depend on us for so much, keeping the memories alive is also part of our responsibility as a parent; try to capture all of the great ones, especially the milestones and celebrations. It is crucial to raising happy, healthy, well-adjusted kids. Memories are where stories are born, relationships are built and family trees and legacies develop and grow.

Now I see why so many moms, especially stay-at-home moms (because they have more time) spend so much time scrapbooking, because these memories are so vital to healthy growth and development. Scrapbooking is a creative skill that I wish I had acquired or had the time to pursue. I have hoards of pictures that I have saved and said I would scrapbook when I get the time, but that day is still yet to come.

There are many ways to keep the memories alive, even if you don't scrapbook. As long as you have pictures, videos, etc., you can review them whenever you want. You can keep memories alive by having a conversation while driving in the car and reliving certain events, talking while having dinner, while waiting in line, waiting in the doctor's office, riding on the plane, watching a sports game on TV, cleaning the house or doing other chores. I can always find time to cherish the memories and relive certain moments in time with dialogue and laughter. All it takes is a lot of "remember whens".

Although I was divorced and my daughter's dad decided to no longer participate as an active parent in her life, I still felt it was important to make sure she had positive memories of a time when he was involved in her life, and remind her that he loved her. Even to this day as I begin writing this book, I still remind her of how he used to fight with me to give her a bath when she was an infant and how his face lit up when she was born and anytime she was in his presence. I also show her videos and pictures of special moments and holidays they shared while he was present and involved in her life. I want her to understand that just because he has some demons in his life that he has to deal with, it does not mean he doesn't love her. He just does not know how to love himself enough to love anyone else fully.

We have taken many family trips, just the two of us. We take local trips to the museum, the zoo, parks, beaches and to festivals. We may spend a night or two in a hotel downtown in our city, go for long drives as well as trips to fun places; Disney World in Florida, California, Chicago to visit family, and Caribbean cruises. We are always taking pictures or making videos, something to capture the memories we are constantly creating.

Yes, we travel a lot, but I have always found economical ways to travel. Some may say, "Well money is tight and entertainment and travel is too expensive." Find ways to save and stash away extra money just for this purpose, even if just for once a year or once every two years. There are always deals that you can find if you research extensively via the internet and word of mouth.

Network with others in the community. Ask around and obtain feedback from others that may have resources or inexpensive travel ideas that they have done with their family. Today, there is even a company Groupon.com that offers many values and promotions on anything from travel vacations, meals at restaurants, spa treatments and entertainment venues such as bowling, go-kart riding, etc. You can even inquire at your local credit union or your company's human resources department for savings coupons and vacation savings accounts. When my daughter was younger, we traveled most often during off-season times such as at the beginning of the school year after summer break or during hurricane season. These times were not in high demand for most families and I often found much greater discounts on airfare, car rentals, hotels, cruises, attractions, etc.

My daughter would typically be out of school for a few days during an extended Labor Day holiday. We would request homework and school work ahead of time to take with us on our trip and make sure that it was all completed while away and had fun at the same time. This worked out well for many years during her early school-aged years. I must admit, we only were faced with a hurricane once where I made a decision to postpone our cruise after spending a few days in Orlando because it was too scary to be out in the ocean. This happened, fortunately, at the end of her young elementary days when it was still feasible to miss a few days of school.

Have Fun With Your Children While Creating Memories

Take the time to have fun with your children. Cherishing memories begins with, first and most importantly, setting aside quality time to spend with your kids and family to create those memories. As single parents, our lives are so busy because we are doing everything that needs to be done solo, but it is imperative for the growth and development of our children that we spend good, quality time with them creating memories. They do desperately need this, and believe it or not, we do desperately need this, too. We have to force ourselves to do this and find balance and harmony in our lives, even as single parents. You just have to make it happen and stop making excuses. There is always going to be something that we have to do. Life does not stop so that we can do what we have to do. It keeps on moving, with or without us being actively present. You get to choose how you want to live your life and how involved you want to be. Life is too short! We will never get this time back with our children at this age.

Their childhood goes by so quickly; before you know it they are 18 years old or older and going away to college, off to the military or living on their own, and we do not want to waste these precious moments because we will never get them back. So make a commitment to yourself that you will make the time and seize the opportunities, because if you don't, you will certainly regret it.

Once those memories are created and captured either in photos and/or video, you have to regularly re-visit them. This is how you TREASURE memories! Talk about them and feel them, expose the kids to them at various moments. When you are driving, talk about them; while at home preparing dinner, pull out the pictures and reminisce. Memories are wonderful and last a lifetime if you take the time to create them and re-live them consistently, again and again.

(SECRET #9) SUPREME SELF-CARE IS CRITICAL

We as parents spend so much time taking care of others, but how much time do we spend taking care of ourselves? I always knew and felt that you have to take care of yourself so that you can be the "Best You" to take care of your kids. The importance of taking care of myself was taught to me by my mother, and it was also something that I read in parenting books. So naturally, this was a habit I tried to keep on a regular basis as my child was growing up. Sometimes it was easier said than done. As parents, we always seem to be able to take care of our kids and we put everyone else's needs before ours. We need to find ways to unwind, defuse and re-energize to maintain our sanity, especially when there are no dates and no great boyfriend or girlfriend present. Supreme self-care is important so you can be healthy physically, mentally, and spiritually. Each aspect has some effect on the other.

In order to re-energize and take care of yourself, you have to schedule time for yourself intentionally. Schedule "me time" activities in your calendar, just as you would other appointments and important to-do list tasks. This also involves resting and getting enough sleep to restore the mind. Your mind has to be stimulated, but also have times of balance with relaxation and "doing nothing" for great mental health and maintaining focus.

Spiritual and Mental Health are Important

My spiritual fitness is important to me and my well-being, so I have always made it a priority to ensure that we always had a good church at which to worship, pray and commune with other like-minded people no matter where we lived. This has always been important to me as an adult and single parent and it was also an important part of raising my child as a Christian. Spiritual fitness involves being able to tap into a higher source of power. Being spiritually fit helps promote inner drive, purpose, helping with a positive mental attitude towards life, people and events, helps you deal with emotions and stress better, and soothes your mind. You develop your spiritual fitness by making regular times to meditate, pray and connect with your Higher Power on a regular basis, among other things.

In practicing supreme care intentionally, I made sure that I incorporated fun activities into my weekly routine by any means necessary. I would find time whenever I could, while my daughter was in gymnastics or dance classes, visiting with friends, at play dates, at parties, etc. This was my playtime, while she was involved in other activities.. I would take the time to run to the gym and get a quick workout in or stop by and have lunch or dinner with a friend, or get a manicure and/or pedicure depending on how much time I had. As a parent, you have to fit it in where you can, especially as a single parent, and that applies to many, many things—if you get my point (eye wink).

What Brings You Joy? Do You Know?

Do you know what brings you joy? I am not talking about having your children or what brings them joy. What do you do or have done that brings pure, undeniable joy into your soul? I know, it is sometimes difficult for us as parents (especially single parents) to answer this question because we are always giving and providing to others. We can become so consumed in taking care of others that we may not immediately know the answer to this question. We know what brings others joy, but we have not taken the time to know what brings *us* joy.

I read an article several years ago in the O magazine where Oprah talked about making a list of 25 things that bring you joy. This list consisted of things you used to do that brought you pure joy but that you may not be doing anymore, maybe even when you were younger such as riding a bike, skating, bowling, playing games, or watching a sunrise. Whatever you remember doing that stimulates or previously stimulated a joy in your heart and soul. This article was genuinely inspiring and made a huge difference in the quality of my life. I made my own personal list, which has enabled me to remember the things I used to do that brought me joy. Trust me this was not an easy task because I could not remember initially and had to think long and hard about what brought joy in my life besides my daughter.

Presently I make sure to incorporate a few things from this list of 25 things that bring me joy on a daily basis,. Some days it is easier to remember than others.. This helps with spiritual and mental well-being and fitness. I can tell when I am in need of taking care of myself and giving myself a little TLC when my feelings are low, depressed and I am just in a melancholy mood for no reason, or sometimes maybe for a very good reason. I do something simple such as lighting a scented candle, taking a nice relaxing bubble bath while enjoying a delicious glass of white or red wine or even just turning on music that makes me feel good. These are a just a few of the things that bring me joy and are on my list and they may change at different times in my life. You can add more if you like, but try to start off with at least 25 because Oprah said so and it works! Everyone's list is personal although we may share some of the same things. So get started on your list today and see what you come up with.

We all have the tendency to temporarily forget the things we like to do that produces joy within and feeds our spirits when we are so overwhelmed and involved with work, family, surviving, our kids' lives and projects and just dealing with life. Having this list written and kept in a place where I could look at it daily first reminded me that I needed to do something that brought me joy and then it allowed me to remember what things to do that made me feel good that were in the form of taking care of myself. Back then, I tried to incorporate a pleasure from the list into my life at least a few times a week, now I indulge daily.

When indulging in the list of 25, you have to force yourself because it is not a habit to take care of yourself as a parent, let alone a single parent. We are so used to just giving, giving, giving until we are depleted and don't even realize it. We are always taking care of everyone else in spite of ourselves, especially as a woman. We take care of the kids, our parents, our significant other, our jobs, the house, the yard, the groceries, the car; the list can go on and on, but you get the basic point. It is time to start taking care of us. So make your list of 25 things that bring you joy. Take the time and really think about things that you can do instantly, that are not too time consuming and can be done for a few minutes that will bring you joy and allow you to escape and write down as many as possible, up to 25.

As a strict rule this list of 25 things that bring you joy should not include anything that is a chore or a must or should do, but something that is small, takes about 5-10 minutes and brings you pure joy. Keep the list nearby and strive to do one to two things on a daily basis from the list to take care of you. If you forget, then definitely make sure you accomplish something on this list when you are feeling stressed, exhausted and depleted and you need some love. This is the practice of loving yourself.

What is Supreme Self-Care?

Recently, as part of my self-care routine, I participated in coaching sessions that helped me with different aspects of my well-being and staying healthy personally (spiritual, mental, emotional health) and for business (financial health). I have been reminded again that it is extremely important to take care of myself better than I ever have before.. This is what is called supreme self-care. This practice has been so successful that I have also taught my daughter to exercise this type of self-care; she uses it while facing the stresses of college life and growing up. Yes, she has even written down her list of 25 things that bring her joy. It was challenging to her to come up with 25 things because young people don't think in those terms; they just do it. We should be teaching our children this valuable lesson of self-care and getting to know themselves in a deeper, more spiritual and loving manner.

It is a great tool and is beneficial to adults as well as children and teens.

Supreme self-care is crucial at all times but especially as a single parent because you are taking care of everyone else and there is no one taking care of you. You _are_ important, your kids depend on you, but most specifically you are important as a human being and self-care is the greatest form of love of self and others. Remember to always take good care of yourself, because we all teach people how to treat us.

Take Care of Your Physical Health

Supreme self-care also involves staying healthy and physically fit. Make sure you are physically active even if you cannot afford to join a gym; you can do exercise videos at home, take walks after dinner with or without the kids, go to the local park, ride a bike, skate, dance, jog in place at home, do squats, lunges, sit-ups, push-ups, jumping jacks, hula hoop, etc. The point is to maintain good physical activity at least three times a week for a minimum of 20-30 minutes. It is fun to do activities with your children, plus it teaches them healthy habits and also tires them out; a real win-win!

Combine physical activity with a healthy diet that is low in fats, low in sodium and high in fiber from fresh fruits and vegetables on a daily basis, along with adequate consumption of water (a goal of 8 glasses per day) for yourself as well as your children. Make sure you are teaching your children good healthy habits that become a part of a healthy lifestyle because they need to be healthy and energetic and learn these habits at home by the choices of food that are available from infancy. Staying active, eating healthy and maintaining good spiritual and mental health are all interrelated and can boost your energy and stamina, which you really need as a single parent who is doing it all.

Now that my daughter is no longer at home and away in college, I am faced with a completely different set of other life changes. No, the empty nester syndrome is not just for married people; you really do experience it as a single parent. Imagine, you are used to being a parent and doing it all and then suddenly there is not much to do. You go instantly from one extreme to the other. Suddenly all the kids are gone and you are alone in the house—no husband, just you. Believe me it is a whole other *major* life adjustment. This is when, if you have been practicing supreme self-care all along, it helps to make this adjustment a little easier However, it does not take it away completely. Time to take it up a notch and learn to treat yourself better than you ever have before and enjoy!!!

(SECRET #10) TO DATE OR NOT TO DATE: A CHOICE TO MAKE AS A SINGLE PARENT

Are you concerned about dating as a single parent? To date or not to date? That is the question. One component of taking care of yourself involves your dating life. As a single parent, I did not realize how complicated this would be. This was not something that was of immediate importance or part of my thought process as I was dealing with the failure of my marriage, but I had no idea of the challenges I would embrace later on in the process of dating.

Challenges of Dating as a Single Mother

Dating as a single parent presents so many pressures. Single mothers face the most challenges. First, there are men these days that like to prey on single moms because they believe they are easy and desperate for love and attention. There are also men that believe that single women are so busy that they do not have to commit their time and themselves completely to the relationship. This can be a win/win situation for a man that is commitment phobic, but not an ideal situation for a single mother who needs more consistency.

Other challenges involve keeping your children safe and protected from child predators. At times, these dangerous types of people may target single parents because they believe they are busy and not as attentive to their children. Some predators will target single women to date, or even marry them, to have access to the children. Single parents have to decipher who is legitimately interested in them as the adult and not in their children. There are a lot of incidences where people have been molested as children and where they were molested in their own home from someone that the child and their parents trusted completely. This can happen to both female and male children. Child molesters are sick and twisted and it is our duty and desire as parents to protect our children. This was the greatest threat that kept me from dating much when my child was younger. I was determined to do everything in my power to prevent this from happening as she grew up.

I attempted to navigate the dating world when my

daughter was younger, but I quickly learned how distrusting I was of having males in my home where I felt we were most vulnerable. I was paranoid of anyone being in the house with my daughter, even if I felt that I knew him. I remember having a boyfriend that I had been dating for a while. He started to come over in the evenings after I had put my daughter to sleep or would stay after we all had gone out to dinner to hang out. The house that I lived in at the time was considered a raised ranch where you had the lower level "basement" or family room area and the top level was the main level where the bathrooms and bedrooms were. To this day, he has no idea that whenever he went upstairs to the bathroom, I monitored the amount of time he was up there and turned the television down to listen to his footsteps to make sure that his steps were not leading to my daughter's bedroom. When I felt he was taking too long to do his business in the bathroom, I was upstairs to find out what he was doing. He was almost always in the bathroom; on occasion, I caught him preparing snacks to bring down or even repairing something that needed to be fixed, and I was relieved.

I never felt guilty or ashamed of my behavior but it got to be extremely stressful for me and I had to finally make a decision that I could not have men in the house when my daughter was home. I would go out and date when my mother would babysit or when my daughter spent the night out with family or friends. I also eventually had a bathroom installed in the lower level so no one would have a reason to go upstairs to use the bathroom while visiting. This helped to ease some of the stress and paranoia.

At times I did regret that I did not make more of an effort to date when my daughter was younger because maybe I would have re-married. Maybe I could have given her a second opportunity to have a father figure in her life.. This is the only regret I have about not trying harder to deal with my fears and allow someone else to be a part of both of our lives. She will never be able to relive her childhood and have the experience of having a father in her life to love her, care for her, and make her feel loved, special and beautiful in only a way that a father or father figure can. This is something she will never have and something I can never give her now. I sometimes wonder if things could have been different if I had opened up my heart and life and allowed someone else in. I will never know, but I do take some respite in knowing that maybe I did prevent something awful from happening.

I will say that the choice to date or not is a personal one. Choosing not to date was a personal decision that I felt was best for us both at the time.

It is Important for Children to Witness Healthy Relationships

I believe it is important for your children to see you engaged in healthy, loving relationships with someone romantically. It is wonderful for them to witness because it teaches them about healthy relationships and what to look for when they begin to socialize, and then later, date. This is important for teen boys and especially girls. It is also great for them to see you involved with healthy friendship relationships so that as they get older and *you do* start dating it is easier for them to digest. If you wait too long, they become so possessive of you, your time and attention that they are unwilling or initially incapable or accepting having to share you with someone else. They may feel betrayed by you or afraid that someone else is more important than they are and that their relationship with you is going to change and become irrelevant. We as adults know this is not true, but in their minds it is possible and will need to be addressed.

This was a reality that I was forced to have to deal with when I started to date again. My daughter was a little older and a freshman in high school (yes, a freshman in high school) and she wanted me to date. Or so she thought. But when it actually happened, it was a totally different situation.

When the guy I was dating would visit, she would distance herself and go to her room. I would invite her to watch TV or hang out with us but she would refuse. Initially, when I questioned her about it, she would say she was fine with him being here and that she liked him. I later found out she was extremely uncomfortable with him being in our lives when I received a letter she wrote me and left it in my bedroom for me to find after he left our house one evening. I still have the letter. She basically informed me that she wanted me to be happy and she is glad that I have someone in my life, she did not want to be selfish, but that it seemed as if he was going to take her place. She was worried that I would not love her anymore (or less) because he was now in my life. She said she knew it may sound crazy, but that was how she felt because she had never seen me in a relationship with a guy I liked. She was not used to it, and it would take her some time to get used to it because it was extremely awkward for her. She wrote that she hoped I would not be mad at her but that this was how she was feeling and that she was sorry.

I had suspected that this was probably how she was feeling in some manner, but not to that extent, because I felt I was doing all that I could to include her in order to prevent these feelings. What I was doing or not doing was not the issue. The issue stemmed from the fact that I had not provided opportunities in the past for her to actually witness me in healthy, serious and intimate heterosexual relationships. This was unfamiliar territory and she had no idea what to expect. I made the decision early on, to sacrifice having various "boyfriends" in and out of her life, but I waited too long and neglected this important lesson and opportunity of demonstrating what good, healthy, intimate relationships should look like.

Your Children Are the Priority. Don't Introduce Them to Everyone You Date

When and if you decide to date, set expectations with yourself as well as with your children. Reassure them that they are important and number one in your life. Listen and take into consideration their feelings about the person you are dating once you decide to introduce this person into their lives. Wait until you are sure this person meets your expectations, that he or she is open and loving and will be accepting of your children as your priority, and that they are safe to bring around your children.

Be sure to keep spending individual time with your children so they know they are important to you, while you gradually allowing them to spend more time together with you and your new significant other. Take it slow and don't rush or force your children to like this new person right away. Allow them to express their feelings and really listen, hear and accept how they feel. Look at it from their perspective and put yourself in their shoes. Try to understand how they feel without being judgmental.

Everyone must decide which route they will take regarding whether to date or not, but like all choices that you make in life, it comes with sacrifices. As I mentioned in previous chapters, good, active parenting involves making choices that are best for your family as a whole.

(SECRET #11) SINGLE PARENTS CAN BE FINANCIALLY RESPONSIBLE AND HEALTHY!

As a single parent, do you worry about money, money, money? Do you become stressed every time you sit down to pay the bills? Finances are important in any household. Depending on your status when you become a single parent, the financial implications can be significant and harsh. If you were once married and accustomed to living with the fruits of a two parent household, income then making an adjustment one salary will be challenging, but necessary and doable. You may find yourself in the position of having to make some quick and essential lifestyle adjustments. You may have always just depended on your one salary and now have to make adjustments to accommodate more than just yourself or an increased number of children while parenting solo. Whatever the situation, a budget is important and practical to being financially responsible and secure. Having a budget helps you become intentional about your finances and spending.

Being financially responsible is critical as a single parent because you have no one else to depend on. It is just your one income, or two if you have more than one job, but it is still only you, making the cheddar and bringing home the bacon. The family depends on you because you are the head of the household and your children depend on you to show them how it is done; they are always watching and usually repeat behaviors they see you demonstrate. So you need to get started and the best place to start is with a budget. This is your financial blueprint to discover where you are financially and where you need to go.

Budgeting Basics…How to Get Started

To start, your budget you must initially keep track of all of your spending for about a month. That means that every penny you spend should be accounted for (at least as much as possible) for accuracy. If you have a bank account, this may be easier to accomplish by using your bank card or debit card for all purchases because you have a statement available to you online and you can actually see exactly where every penny is spent. This is an advantage of using online banking at your bank of choice. This will give you a clear picture of what you are actually spending your money on, including bills and essentials as well as non-essentials such as entertainment, restaurants, shopping or anything else.

The second step is to make a list of all your required household expenses. In the list you should include: mortgage or rent payments, all insurance payments, credit card payments, childcare costs, utilities, homeowners association fees, and car payments. Total all of these payments for the month. Next, list your non-essential spending such as entertainment, dining, cleaners, clothes shopping, hair appointments, etc. This is the list of all the extras.

Third step is to make a list of all of your income including employment wages, bonuses, government assistance, alimony, child support (only if it is consistent) and total all of this for the month.

The fourth step in the process is to deduct your total expenses from your total income. Start this initially with your required or essential expenses. This will provide a clear picture of where your financial strengths and weaknesses are, including where you need to make adjustments and what to cut back on. Undergoing this process and developing a budget will provide a framework or blueprint of your financial "health".

The reason you don't list child support if it is not consistent is because you cannot depend on something that is not constant. This will only make you frustrated, stressed, angry and short on finances that you were expecting at the end of the month. Let these extra sporadic payments be a "bonus" that you can utilize for future savings and/or for a rainy day, emergency stash, or for family extras. The point is, if it is not consistent, then don't become dependent on it. This will cut down on stress in your life.

Initially you might not have enough income coming in (even with the sporadic child support payments coming in) to start a savings or emergency fund, but this should be your ultimate goal once you start to have your basic needs and expenses met financially. Emergencies are a part of life and will present themselves when you least expect it and can least afford it. It is always wise to start building an emergency fund, even if it is just $500-$1,000. It will continue to grow if you touch it only for true emergencies and not for getting your hair done, for an outing on the town, or a loan to a family member. These are not emergencies.

There are many free budget tools that you can find online such as mint.com,, online banking institution, and free apps on your smart phone that you can download and utilize. Research and find the budgeting tool that is appropriate for you and offers you the most simplicity so that you will be more apt to use it.

When you are on a strict budget you will have to find ways to entertain yourself and your children for free. Trust me, depending on where you live, there are many free activities that you can find in your town or surrounding towns. Investigate, and I challenge you to find at least 5-10, or more. Challenge your children to help you find free activities that interest them, as well. Get them involved in the process and make it a fun adventure.

Resources to Help with Struggling Budgets

If you are struggling financially, there are many resources that are available to parents with children. There is temporary government assistance available to help with providing food for your family, reduced housing, healthcare, assistance with childcare so that you can work, job placement, etc. Contact your local state social services for assistance and guidance regarding the various types of temporary programs that are available such as:

- Temporary Assistance for Needy Families (TANF)
- Temporary Assistance for Needy Families – Unemployed Parents (TANF-UP)
- Food Stamps, Medicaid for Families and Children
- Medical Need Programs

Take the time to check online for the websites and locations of these and other services available. There are also several federal programs and other resources listed below that offer assistance to single parent families.

Federal Programs:

The Department of Health and Human Services (HHS) administers a wide range of federal programs for families and children. HHS has regional offices throughout the country that provide access to services.

Department of Health and Human Services, Administration for Children and Families

370 L'Enfant Promenade, S.W. Washington, DC 20447

202/401-9215

www.acf.hhs.gov/

The Children's Defense Fund is a national child advocacy organization dedicated to helping children and their families. Check their website for information on a variety of programs, including Head Start, Safe Start and Fair Start.

>	Children's Defense Fund
>	25 E. Street, NM, Washington, DC 20001
>	202/628-8787
>	www.childrensdefense.org

Other programs offered by the Children's Defense Fund include Head Start, Safe Start and Fair Start. All three programs work to ensure that children grow up in safe homes, schools and neighborhoods.

Parents Without Partners, Inc. --- is a resourceful website that provides single parents and their children with opportunities for enhancing personal growth, self-confidence and sensitivity towards others by offering an environment for support, friendship and the exchange of parenting techniques.

The link is: www.parentswithoutpartners.org

While you work through this, you may come to the conclusion that you need additional skills and/or education to obtain a better paying job to cover expenses.

If you are interested in returning to school to gain higher education, the first step is to fill out the Free Application for Federal Student Aid, also known as FAFSA. This can be found online at the website www.fafsa.ed.gov and will determine what your financial needs are and if you qualify for government subsidized student aid (grants and lower interest government student loans to assist with tuition payment, books, and other college financial needs). Colleges and universities also use this information to qualify you for scholarships available at their respective campuses. Search online for other scholarship opportunities, but be extremely careful and wary of the many scams out there. Don't send any money or offer any of your or your children's personal information online without thorough research to make sure the company or offer is legitimate.

There is financial assistance available to help with payment of tuition and fees and may also cover book expenses, childcare and transportation at various schools. Evening classes are available after work, as well as online classes. Schools offer financial assistance for single parents that are in financial need with scholarships and grants that do not need to be paid back. The point is there are many options and resources at your disposal to help struggling single parents advance their education and labor skills; you just have to seek them out and ask the appropriate questions.

You may also have to consider taking on an extra job part-time to bring in additional income. Maybe you can start a home-based business such as childcare services for other parents that need assistance and are able to pay. You might have a hobby or special talent such as baking, cooking, gift baskets, party planning, decorating, sewing, cosmetology, organizing, housekeeping, virtual assistance, graphic design, etc. Turn that skill into a profitable home-based business!

Other Tips to Reduce Spending:

Sometimes we are still "just short" of the needed cash. What has worked for myself and other single mothers is to de-clutter and sell the extra things you no longer need or use at garage sales and consignment shops. You can also use online selling sites such as eBay and Amazon. You can find treasures at garage sales that you can also resell for a higher price to receive a profit.

When there are simply more bills and expenses than money coming in, you have to get creative with shopping and spending. Find ways to reduce expenses with grocery shopping such as searching for and using online coupons, which are abundantly available. Coupons are also found in the newspapers and on bulletin boards in the grocery stores you shop at. Seek out inexpensive housing and ways of co-habitation with other single parent family members or friends; this can be a win-win for both by offering an opportunity to share expenses and assist each other with childcare arrangements. This can start off as a temporary solution until you get on your feet, or it can work out surprisingly well for the long term.

Learn to live with less and spend money only on things you absolutely need. Many of us, including myself, are at times guilty of too much impulse buying and unnecessary spending. Most times, if we really evaluate our spending, we will find that a lot is being spent on too many things that are "wants" (such as iPads, expensive cars, video games, name brand purses, shoes and clothes, things we really cannot afford) vs. "needs" which are essential and necessary (such as food, housing, electricity, childcare, a reliable, economical car, etc.). Begin asking yourself, "Do I want this or is it truly a need?" Seek out economical ways to buy basic clothes and outfits, look for sales shops and thrift stores, as they have a lot of nice inexpensive vintage clothing that is also stylish. Spend money only on what is essential and necessary for the survival of you and your children until you can start making more money. Sometimes we have to satisfy wants, but make sure needs are met first.

When you are able to begin saving some of your income, start by paying yourself first, by putting away money in a savings vehicle. 10% is the goal, but start where you can. 1%, 2% or even just $25-$50 a month accumulates and you end up with more than you started with at the end of the year. Have money directly deposited into an account if possible so it's never accessible for you to spend.

Begin to save for your emergency fund of at least 6 months of living expenses in case of job loss, illness, household issues, etc. when possible. Save extra money received either in sporadic child support payments, gifts, bonuses at work, etc. Also, set aside a small fund to treat yourself and your children to special treats such as movies and other entertainment, restaurant outings, and family trips at least once a year.

Seek out and utilize all the help that is available from friends, family, church, government agencies, and your community, and set a goal to make it temporary so that you don't become dependent on it. Leave some for the next person that may be struggling and need a little assistance to get back on their feet or who just needs a fresh start. Abuse is rampant and causing burden and concern about whether or not to keep these resources available, and we all want them available to help someone who is really in need. So, don't abuse it. You want to be able to pay it forward and help your fellow sisters or brothers who need assistance and support, right? What a joy it is to reach out and assist someone else in the same manner that someone once assisted you!

One of the most valuable money lessons my father taught me early in life was to live as debt free as possible. Avoid bad debt, especially credit card debt, and if you have debt, pay it off and keep if off. He used to always say: "If you can't afford it, don't buy it" and "if you cannot pay off the card at the end of the month, then don't use it."

What helps combat bad debt situations is to save money for big price purchases, especially those that are wants and not needs. If you use credit cards, pay off the total at the end of each billing cycle when due. Don't use credit cards as a loan because the interest is high and it takes forever paying them off, especially if you only pay the minimum amount. You could end up paying three, four, five times more than the actual cost of what the purchases were once interest and fees are added together. Once you find yourself in debt, it is challenging to get out, so the best thing is to try avoiding it in the first place, if at all possible.

Make sure you pay your bills on time, including utilities, etc. If you are unable to pay then call the company and establish a payment plan, don't just ignore your bills and debts. Companies are willing to work with you if you ask and attempt to negotiate. Not paying bills and obligations timely greatly affects your credit rating and credit worthiness in a negative manner, making it difficult to obtain credit initially and also making it difficult to qualify for the best rates when buying a car, furniture, insurance, a house and getting a mortgage loan or even a rental. Some people don't realize the damage that not paying bills and debt in a timely manner can cause until it is too late and they are denied opportunities.

Timely payment of bills and incurred debt is the benchmark of how credit is judged and determined. Unpaid bills become late and delinquent when not paid as agreed upon, and then turn into debt that becomes unmanageable and before you know it, you are spiraling into credit problems. Negative credit can make it difficult to get school loans and may even affect your chances of getting your dream job or career. Debt can be quick and easy to get into, but difficult and time consuming to get out of, and the process can take many years. So be wise, careful, responsible and accountable with your bills and other financial obligations.

Your Health is Your Wealth

Keeping yourself healthy is also an important aspect of your finances. Your health is your wealth, in every sense of the word. Good health is a valued asset. You need good health to effectively work a job or career every day, take care of the kids and actively participate in life. Good health means decreased insurance premiums and medical bills that can destroy family finances. It is more economical to live a healthy lifestyle than an unhealthy one with smoking, excessive drinking, gambling, overeating, etc. All of these habits can be expensive, especially over time. Have you seen the price of cigarettes? Let alone the physical damage it does to your body? Take care of your physical health, because it can and will adversely affect your financial health if you don't.

Don't be afraid or too proud to ask for help if and when you need it, because one day you will be in a better position to help yourself and at some point maybe even help someone else by paying it forward. We all need help once in a while and it is nothing to be ashamed of.

Child Support

Only one third of single mothers receive any child support, and the average amount these mothers receive is only about $300 a month. Even fewer fathers receive child support from the mother when they are ordered to pay; it's not just fathers not paying child support and being a "deadbeat" parent. This is why it is recommended to not include this in your budget unless it is consistently supplied as required and court ordered by a judge.

If you are not receiving child support and/or don't have a child support order, you need to start the process of filing for child support as soon as possible by contacting your local state Office of Child Support Enforcement Agency. This service is free, but in some states there may be a small administrative fee, and they will assist you with the process even if the other parent resides in another state or you are not sure of their location. If you are going through a divorce, ensure that an order is placed with the judge in the paperwork when the divorce is granted to decrease costs of returning to court for this order at a later date, because it will cost some money. Once child support is ordered, you will have additional financial support for child-related expenses like food, shelter, clothing, medical care, child care, education, transportation, entertainment and other activities. Check your local Attorney General Child Support Division from your state for more information.

The Attorney General's Child Support Division has a responsibility to assist parents in obtaining the financial support necessary for children to grow up and succeed in life. To encourage parental responsibility, the Attorney

General establishes paternity of children and court orders for financial and medical support, and vigorously enforces support orders. The Attorney General promotes the emotional involvement of both parents in the life of the child by working with community groups, schools and hospitals.

(SECRET #12) A CHILD'S NEEDS ARE TRULY SIMPLE, BUT WE MAKE IT COMPLICATED

Kids' needs are very simple. They just want to know and feel that they are loved and cared for, that they are safe, secure, and that someone has "got their back". No matter how a child is acting out, this behavior mostly stems from the fact that their needs are not being met. A baby cries because they cannot communicate their needs yet. You have to figure out what they need, and when you do, they stop crying. The same is true with older children; although they can talk, they still don't know how to communicate a lot of the feelings and emotions that are going on inside of them. Even us, as adults, still frequently have a difficult time expressing our emotions and feelings to others. Yet, we expect our children to be fluent in this area and we have not even taught them how to do it. Instead, because they are frustrated, impatient and don't know what else to do, their emotions come out in negative behaviors and they feel that we just don't "get them" or understand them. Most times, we don't. There are things you can do to help them calm down and learn to express their emotions in a positive manner.

When my daughter was younger, we purposely named the loveseat in our living room the "Love Couch". It was a consciously chosen symbol. When she needed love, we would go to the love couch and cuddle and she would tell me what was bothering her. She learned to just say "I need a hug" or "I need some love" and she knew she could expect to get it. No matter what I was doing at the time, I would stop it immediately, or if I was finishing something quickly I would say "give me a quick minute" and would finish what I was doing so that I could give her the attention she needed at the time. I knew this was something huge for her, yet so small for me to do.

When kids are acting out emotionally, it is usually about not getting attention or needing some attention, love and hugs. Instead of acting out, I taught her to say, "Can you meet me at the love couch?" or simply "I need some love, Mom" or "I need a hug". This seemed to blunt a lot of acting out on her part and it was good for me, too, because sometimes I did not know that I also needed a little "love". It was nice to take a break, to re-energize and focus on my child.

Teach Children About Their Emotions

We, as adults, have a difficult time expressing our emotions, so just imagine how difficult it is for our children. We have to teach them about the many emotions that are flooding into them such as love, anger, sadness, disappointment, fear, envy, loneliness, joy, etc. They need to learn to recognize them by name and know that they are just feelings and will pass. We need to give them the necessary tools to identify them and then know what to do or not to do when they experience these feelings. This is part of teaching healthy and unhealthy behaviors and will assist with preventing and cutting down on some of the negative "acting out" behavior that is frustrating for both the parent as well as the child. This will be discussed more in the Chapter of Discipline.

Sometimes, we can get so caught up in our schedules with work and in the world of craziness that is going on in our daily lives that we don't even take time for ourselves, let alone our children, and they really need some of our time. Some of our undivided, fully focused and engaged time. It does not take a lot of time; after about

10-15 minutes she was usually feeling energized and loved and was ready to go back to what she was doing. Sometimes it was longer. At times I found it was also what I needed to end my workday or to get off the phone from a long conversation and calm myself down and unwind.

Children need us to teach them how to love and honor themselves as human beings and children of God that are worthy and deserve love, respect, safety, security, honor, and to be taken care of. Our children need to know their worth, that they are valuable and important. This is really critical with children of single parents because they may have innate feelings of abandonment because of the absent parent and need to know that their self worth is not tied to anyone. We need to show love, compassion, and show our kids what healthy confidence and self-esteem look like by mirroring it as a reflection of who we are and how we live our lives. Be mindful of the words you say to your children so as not to tear them down but to build them up with confidence and esteem.

Children Need to Know They Are Worthy and Loved

It is crucial to do whatever is in your power to teach your children that they are worthy. Regardless of whether their mother or father decided to be a part of their lives, it is not because they are unworthy as children, and it has nothing to do with them because they are amazing. It has everything to do with the absent parent being irresponsible, sick, and/or fighting their own issues of worth, responsibility and whatever other demons may be present. The absent parent has no idea or does not realize how wonderful of a child they have or what they are missing out on; it is the absentee parent's loss. The child's worth is based upon who God created them to be and He loves them exponentially. He created them because they are important, have value, worth, and are truly blessed with something wonderful to offer this world and the universe. Teach them that God has magnificent things planned for them and He truly love them.

It is important to constantly repeat these words of empowerment, encouragement and self-worth to your children until they fully believe and understand how amazing, important, loved and worthy they are from the time they are small children until they are young adults and beyond. We all need to be reminded of how wonderful and significant we are, as well as how loved we are by our parents, close friends, family and God. That our mere existence in this world is not by accident, but we are supposed to be here; our presence is on purpose because God has a marvelous and magnificent plan for us and He loves us more than we will ever know.

Kids Are People Too, So Consider Their Needs

Because growing up is already so difficult, make sure you consider how the decisions you make in life will affect your children. We need to constantly remind ourselves that kids are actually people too, just miniature size. We have to respect them as little people with feelings about what happens to them and their lives, and give them the same type of loving respect as we would any other human. Sometimes we have to make major life-changing decisions that not only affect us, but may have a life-altering effect on your children as well, so you really have to be mindful of this and include them in the decision making. You want them to know that how they feel matters. This empowers them and makes them feel important and valued.

When my daughter was between the ages of 10 and 12, I had been talking to family and friends about my desire to move back to Houston at some point because I truly enjoyed living there. The reason I moved back to Chicago was not because my marriage was failing, but because my father was terminally ill with cancer and I wanted to spend more time with him, and also allow him to spend more time with his granddaughter so they could get to know one another. I always had the intent to move back to Houston at some point after his death.

When my daughter was 12 years old and about to enter 7th grade, I immediately decided it was either now or never. Either I could move now or I would have to wait until after she finished high school because I would not have her go through a traumatic move while in the middle of it. I felt she was still young, but right at the cusp where she could still adjust easily and make new friends.

I included her in the decision and discussed it with her before making my final decision. She was a little nervous but felt that if this was what I wanted then she would be OK with it. She thought it would be fun to make new friends. I made a deal with her that we both had to enjoy living in Houston. If after the first year she did not like it or had not adjusted adequately, we would move back to Chicago, that way she would be in 8th grade and would move to the new high school with already established friends and would have an easier adjustment. I did not want her to move after high school had started because I felt it would not be fair to her and it would be more stressful the older she was. We made the plans and within 3 months, we were moving to Houston.

It was an adjustment for both of us. Things were not as I had planned, but once we were in Houston and settled neither one of us wanted to make the trek back to Chicago, so we learned to make the necessary adjustments. To this day, she still is not in love with Houston, but I provided her the opportunity to feel empowered because she was included in a major decision that she was also affected by. It was a huge move from one state to another but it was a successful transition because I allowed her to be a part of the decision making process and she felt important, cherished and valued. Because of this, she also wanted to cooperate and work as a team. Children act out most when they feel disconnected and as if their opinions and feelings don't matter, aren't acknowledged, or they don't have an opportunity to weigh in or be heard. Of course, at times an opposite decision may still have to be made, but when appropriate explain to them the reasons why. Sometimes it may simply be, "because I said so". They may need to be told after a final decision is made that they did not agree with, "You may not understand it or like it, but I have definitely taken your feelings into consideration and hopefully we can come to a compromise and work together as a team because I really need you to support me on this one." We all know that the parent is in charge and has the final say, but allow your children to feel valued and listened to, and acknowledge their feelings throughout the process.

As a parent, you have the most important job. Yes, it is more important than your job that you clock into from 9-5 (although that job is very important and necessary). Your children, their safety and well-being is *most* important. You can go to jail for not being there for your kids, and face the possibility of losing them in so many ways. Yes, you will get fired and have to find another job for not showing up for work, but you will be free to roam around and find another one and still have your kids and their unconditional love.

You, as the solo parent, are responsible for creating a strong and solid foundation for your children to develop from. No excuses! You are your child's first role model and maybe the only one for a while. They are depending on us as their solo parent, and society is depending on us, as well, to do right by our children and be active, engaged parents. Our kids did not ask to be born into this world; we as parents made the choices that produced offspring. We created them and now we owe them our very best!

(SECRET #13) CHILDREN PROVIDE THE SUPREME GIFT OF UNCONDITIONAL LOVE, IF WE JUST ALLOW THEM

Being a mom, I have pleasantly discovered that children are the most loving, precious gifts from God, and they can love you better than anyone else can in your life. Pay attention to how they love you when they are young, and appreciate it. A child's love is unconditional; they love you no matter what and "just because". They love you when you are looking your worst, smelling your worst, acting your worst, even when you mistreat them- they still love you. They always want to be with you and never want to leave you. You can do no wrong in their eyes when they are young. They just love you. That is the best kind of love to me, no strings attached, just free, effortless love. That was enough for me at the time and I never knew that I could experience the type of love I feel in my heart for my daughter, as well. My heart swells up and is so full of love that is so beautiful, effortless, joyous, and difficult to describe in words alone, but it brings a smile to my face and heart with just so much joy!

You may feel episodes of loneliness whether you are or are not in a relationship. You may also feel unloved, unworthy and guilty. Guilt is huge with solo parents because we cannot always provide in the manner that we want for our children. We may feel guilty about breaking up the household if our marriage or relationship did not work out, or feel responsible for the current situation our family is in.

Slow Down and Take Time to Experience the Power of Unconditional Love

We, as single parents, can be really tough on ourselves and can get stuck in negative feelings often. But if you make a habit of just being still, meditating, paying attention and becoming fully aware, you will see and feel the love that is all around you. As a single parent, I often felt so overwhelmed, distracted by all of the many tasks and responsibilities, that most times I discovered I was living in a sleep-like state. I was not fully aware of the love that was always surrounding me. I was on autopilot at times and just trying to get it all done. Until you can force yourself to slow down, unwind, meditate and pray, you are living day to day unconsciously and just going through the motions. It also prevents you from enjoying the simple pleasures, being fully engaged in life and fully present with your children.

This is when you need to practice supreme self-care as discussed earlier in the book and also let your kids love you. Children love us so much and love to hug and love on us. Receive their love because it is good, authentic, pure love and it is unconditional. It is also so energizing and can restore you instantly when you feel depleted.

I am dismayed at times when I am in a public setting and observe children attempting to love their parents and the parents push them away or scold them. You can see the desperation in their little eyes and the need for affection that they crave from their parents. These same parents don't realize that they desperately need to be loved, as well. Sometimes, we may be seeking love from someone else (a man or woman that does not seem to care) and we do not realize that the love we need may be right in front of us, the unconditional love that your children can dote on you. It may not be the kind of intimacy that we sometimes translate to mean "love", but it is the pure unconditional love that children give you just because. That is the supernatural kind of powerful, spiritual love!

Children, in return need to feel loved, important, cherished and secure. Their needs are really simple. Unconditional love feels wonderful to receive, but it is something that we should always strive to provide to our children in return. It is a love that should be reciprocated. Children inherently have it and are born with it. This kind of love, this unconditional love, is powerful and transformational. Our children need to feel this in good times and bad times, when they are nice and also when they are naughty.

Children Are Born Loving Unconditionally; Keep it Growing

Sometimes parents tend to hold back their love from their children when they are upset with them or when the children have done something that is unacceptable. When we do this, we teach our children that our love is conditional, that our love is given only when they are doing well, being obedient and/or being perfect little angels. Children need to know and truly feel that we love them all of the time and that there is nothing they can do, nothing they can say and no physical appearance will make us love them less because they are perfect in our eyes.

It is our responsibility as parents to teach our children that their actions are not tied to whether or not we love them. Children need to understand that behavior and actions have nothing to do with loving them or whether or not they love us. Our love will not be taken away or granted depending on their actions or behavior. This will set the foundation early on with children that love is not earned. It will help them to avoid becoming people pleasers. People-pleasing is a challenging behavior that is difficult to overcome; some people are prone to this and sometimes for the rest of their lives. It is learned behavior that can start in childhood.

Children inside the womb love their mother purely and unconditionally as they are developing, before they are even born. The love is already there, and we, as humans, are born with it. This wonderful love continues after birth through childhood. Fathers become the recipient, as well, if they are present. We as parents have to nurture this natural and supreme gift of unconditional love. We have to accept it, enjoy it, model it and return it back to our children. It is truly a splendorous gift and we should appreciate it as such.

COMMUNICATION

(SECRET #14) "DO AS I SAY, NOT AS I DO" DOES NOT WORK!

Kids learn from watching what you do (your actions and your words) and they are always watching. Some older folks used to always say, "Do as I say, not as I do." Have you ever heard that phrase? It is very familiar in many households, passed on from generation to generation. A lot of us have heard or witnessed this phrase being repeated and acted upon in our lifetimes. I know it was popular in my childhood days. Back in those days, parents and grandparents expected their kids to literally watch them cut up, act out, get drunk, fight, curse people out, treat others with disrespect, have different men and women in and out of the house, and still never repeat the negative behaviors they witnessed.

The phrase "Do what I say, not as I do" implies to a child that, as a parent, I can do whatever I want, act crazy and all but I hold you to a different standard. You can witness my outlandish behavior but you better not repeat it. You just better do what I say. This is such a double standard because we as parents, and our child's role model may fail to demonstrate acceptable behavior, but expect them to do so, without seeing it from us because we "said so".

When I was a child I always believed that this concept did not make sense. I could not comprehend this type of adult thinking. As an adult, I know without a doubt that this is contradictory behavior and expectations. Children learn from watching their parents, guardians, teachers and other authority figures. You, as a parent, are your child's mentor. If you don't teach them appropriate behavior and consequences of their actions, believe me, society will. There is so much negativity, violence, malice and inappropriate behavior exemplified in our world today. This makes it difficult for children; they have no choice but to learn from the "streets" if they don't have a stable foundation of love, exemplary behavior and discipline at home to learn from. This is what we don't want for our children.

Your kids watch what you do continuously. When your actions and words are consistently mix-matched, it makes it challenging for children to believe your or take you seriously. They may soon determine that you are a fraud, a fake, or a phony and lose respect for you. Yes, you are an adult and there are many things adults are allowed to do that children cannot because of their age. But allow them to witness you doing these things responsibly and with discretion. You have to get this part right. It is imperative, especially as a single parent, because you are all they have. Your children are watching all that you do, learning from you and your actions, and they are depending on you. Through your behaviors—not just what you say—you are teaching them about trust and integrity.

Divorce Teaches Lessons to Your Child That You Are Not Aware of...

When I divorced my husband, I had no idea there were lessons that I was teaching my daughter: that you cannot let anyone pull you into the gutter with them. No matter how much you love them, you have to love yourself more. You teach people how to treat you. Every adult is responsible for themselves and their actions whether positive or self-destructive. They make decisions when they are in the fork in the road of life that has nothing to do with you, but they can be life-changing decisions for all involved. You choose the road you want to travel and some roads have no U-turn, so be careful about which ones you choose. I had to teach my daughter that sometimes love hurts, but it passes with time. I taught her that after you have done all you can do, then it is time to let go and move on. That I love her and our peace and well-being is most important to me. That I am always here for her and will make sure she is safe mentally, physically and emotionally. That as a woman and mother, she can trust me to make the tough decisions that are in my best interest as well as hers.

Not once did I belittle her dad, talk about him in a negative way or show any disrespect for him in front of my daughter. I wanted her to still feel good about herself as his daughter and that his decisions had nothing to do with how he felt about her, but more about how he lacked love and acceptance for himself. I always told her that he loved her, and to this day, I make sure she has warm memories of sweet things he did for her when she was young how happy he was that she was in the world. It is challenging to build respect when you have the "do as I say, not as I do" attitude. A prime example of this is when children observe their parents smoke cigarettes or get high using marijuana or other drugs or even drink alcohol. These children will have a greater likelihood of experimenting with drugs and repeating the behavior they witnessed while growing up. They grow up and want to try it out, so be ready. Of course, there are exceptions where the opposite will happen, but most often these behaviors are repeated.

Children are Watching What You Do, Always!

When my daughter was younger, I initially started not drinking in her presence or would occasionally have one glass of wine at a party or at a restaurant for dinner. I made a conscious decision to do this. If I had a glass of wine or two at home, it was after her bedtime, when she was sleeping. I also chose to never have a drink in front of her friends when they were over at the house because I never wanted anyone to have the wrong impression based on their limited child-like perspective. I never wanted to be labeled an alcoholic or something. With children, you have to be careful of innocently being called out as "her mom drinks all of the time", etc. They don't know any better, so it is best to keep grown-up business with grown-ups and out of the presence of children as much as possible.

I once overheard a conversation between my daughter and her cousin that went something like this: They were talking about how their life would be as adults and what they would and would not do. The cousin said, "When I grow, up I am not going to drink or smoke." My daughter, on the other hand, said, "When I grow up I am not going to smoke but I will maybe drink a glass of wine sometimes." This blew me away because the cousin's parents don't smoke or drink. This was substantiation that the cousin was emulating learned behavior from her parents. Because my daughter had witnessed my occasional social drinking, this is what she wanted to emulate. Again, there are exceptions to this but for the most part, children will learn from their parents and repeat what they see.

Children really do pay attention to what you are doing, probably more than you think. They do listen to you as well, but your behavior needs to match if you want them to take what you say seriously. I used to always wonder if my verbal messages and lessons were going in one ear and out the other, because you find yourself, as a parent, repeating some of the same messages and talking points to your children. At times, it is like you are a broken record, and you wonder if you are being perceived that way.

I was so delighted the first time I heard my daughter tell her friend and cousin, "Well, my mom says that..." and she shared some of my teachings. I have found her repeating phrases and lessons I have taught her on several occasions. I also heard her cousin recite similar phrases regarding her mother and her teachings. This was so impressive and I was moved to call her mom to share this with her because as parents we don't know if what we are saying is getting through and sticking with our kids. It is immensely comforting and validating to know that your children are really listening, although we may not think they are.

Sometimes it seems like our children are asleep while we are giving them our best "stuff", but we have to keep talking and eventually our words will sink in and become a part of who they are, instilled in them. In order for this to happen, they have to trust and respect you as a parent. They really are listening to us and watching everything we do, so don't sleep on this important reality!

I cannot stress the fact that it all begins in the home. Children are either going to want to grow up and be just like you, or as they grow older, decide they want to be nothing like you from watching your actions. Even if your kids say they don't want to be like you when they grow up, sometimes it is inevitable no matter what. You, as the parent, are the Master Teacher. Your actions are teaching them something about life and how they should behave. Be extremely mindful of what actions you are portraying and make sure they are in alignment with what you are trying to convey to your child verbally, because they are listening *and* watching. Ask yourself: What do my actions teach my child? Am I being consistent with my words and actions? Here is something else to think about as well: If your actions are not in alignment with what you say is right or wrong, what does that tell you about your own decisions and behaviors?

(SECRET #15) OPENNESS AND HONESTY IN COMMUNICATION BUILDS TRUST WITH CHILDREN

Do you ever wonder how effective you are at communicating and getting your points across to your children without tearing them down? Are you concerned about what and how much information you should share with your children? Communication is how we relate to others and it is vital. In order to get things done, we have to learn how to communicate effectively and get our needs met whether in our personal relationships with family and significant others or in business/career. Openness and honesty build trust so that people, including your children, know that you mean what you say and say what you mean.

Unfortunately, we as human beings cannot communicate with telepathy. No one will know what your expectations or desires are unless you communicate them either verbally, in writing, via sign language, or in action. You cannot expect people to read your mind, so you have to practice good, open, honest and clear communication with the people you come into contact with, including your kids. You, as the communicator of information, have the burden to make sure that the deliberate information is transmitted, received and interpreted in the manner you intended.

Honesty in communication and with your actions is something that we all should practice. We are taught this at an early age, in preschool and kindergarten and even in our religious surroundings. I have taught my daughter to be open and honest in communication with everyone, but especially with her closest friends and trusted family members. I have always believed that this is a requirement in any intimate, close, trusting relationship between adults, family members, lovers, friends, employers, children, and so on. The receiver of the information may not always like what you have to say, but it is your responsibility to convey it in a loving, non-threatening and non-judgmental manner.

Teach Children How to Be Honest Without Being Offensive

My daughter was taught to be honest and most people she spends time with knows she is direct. She has lost some friendships over the years because not everyone appreciates her honesty and directness. Sometimes she didn't know how to censor her unsolicited honesty to the appropriate people, in the appropriate manner or at the appropriate time. As a parent, you have to remember that kids take what you say literally and that is the only way they receive information. You have to teach them the process of how to be honest with their friends while also being considerate of how their words come out.

Even in her senior year of high school and freshman year in college, we were still tweaking the "honesty in communication" lesson. For example, she was hanging out with some friends from an organization that she is involved in that decided that they wanted to go and smoke hookah. They took her to a hookah bar while they were out one evening. She had no idea at the time what hookah was, but found out when she arrived at the bar.

The thought of joining her peers and trying it out

crossed her mind, but she decided against it because it did not look appealing and she considered it a form of cigarette smoking, which she already knew the dangers of. Later that night, true to her nature, she did a Google search for hookah on the internet and found many interesting facts and articles discussing the dangers of smoking it. She printed out a few articles and read them to me. The articles said that it was not just flavored vapors as her friends informed her but it had the potential for more long-term damaging effects to the lungs and airways. With good intentions, she decided to share this information with her friends to make them aware of their misconceptions and what the long and short-term consequences were because they informed her that it was harmless and just flavored vapors. She wanted them to have the facts. Well, of course, some of her friends did not appreciate this and felt that she was judging them, being condescending and reprimanding. She came off as trying to be a "know it all", although these were not her intentions at all. Sometimes, perception is reality to others, especially when they doubt your intentions or they don't want to acknowledge something.

She has had a few similar situations happen, even

while in college. I am still explaining this to her and she is finally getting it, that you have to censor what you say at times, and that you cannot always say what you are thinking to everyone, especially unsolicited. It is even difficult to be open and honest with your close friends at times, but you owe them that as a friend or loved one; just say it with love and be ready to deal with the consequences. This does not mean that you are being dishonest. It just means that you are keeping some thoughts to yourself. Not everyone needs to know what you are thinking or what stance you take on a particular matter all of the time. You have to know your audience, who your message is intended for and if they are open to receiving it, so as not to unintentionally offend anyone. Now, if they ask for your opinion and really want you to be honest, then you can do so in a graceful and respectful manner. As long as your intention is not to be mean and cruel when you speak your truth, then speak your truth. Everyone may not like what you have to say or be able to handle it, but people will respect you because they know that you are honest and straightforward.

Yolandra Drake

Good Relationships Are Built on Honesty

While I was separated, before I officially divorced, I tried to date a little, but discovered that this was truly difficult; not just because I was a single mom, but because of the dilemma that I was still legally married. When I first met a guy and he would ask the question, "So, are you married?" I didn't know what to say. If I said, "Yes, I am married but separated" he would sense "drama" and not want to get seriously involved. If I answered, "No, I am not married" I would technically be lying, because even though we had been separated for a few years and he was totally out of the picture, we were still legally married and I would be starting a potential relationship or friendship with a HUGE LIE! I am totally against adults being so deceitful and fraudulent with relationships; this is a pet peeve of mine. I always wondered why so many adults were always intentionally and habitually deceiving one each other, even about small things, when they can do what they want; they are not children. I would have been a huge HYPOCRITE. So I eventually had to get that divorce so that I could go on with my life. I have always believed that how you start a relationship sets the tone for it, so I always wanted to start mine with HONESTY.

HONESTY in communication involves words and action and is so important in any relationship: with your family, friends, co-workers, as well as your children because they are constantly watching you and they learn and repeat what you do, not always what you say. They need to see that your words match your behavior so you are not seen as a hypocrite.

Because children are little people, we need to treat them with respect, kindness and talk to them in the manner in which we want to be spoken to; with love and respect. It is your responsibility to monitor the usage of words that you use to communicate with children while being honest and authentic. Your words can make your children feel loved, safe, protected, confident, strong, powerful, and passionate about life and themselves. However, on the other hand, they can have the opposite effect and leave them feeling broken, torn down, depleted, insignificant, weak, helpless, unstable, unsupported and insecure, among other things.

Communicate With Words of Encouragement and Love

We as parents have to constantly be mindful of how we communicate with our children. We have to choose words that empower them as opposed to words that injure them. Negative words can be damaging and last a lifetime and become implanted in a child's psyche as they grow up. Three words that are the most influential gift that you can give to children are "I love you." This may sound cliché but it is the absolute truth. These three words need to be spoken to your children more than any other words. They should be said with no strings attached, unconditionally, and on a daily basis. The more you say these three beautiful words, the more you and your children will benefit from them. The added bonus is that the more you say them, the more you will also hear them genuinely repeated back to you from your children. "I love you" is precious and should be shown through actions as well as words.

Keep in mind this list of the Ten Most Important Things that you should say to your children often. They are:

1. "I love you."
2. "Do you want _____ or _____? It's your choice."
3. "You can accomplish anything you want."
4. "You are important to me."
5. "There is a solution to every problem."
6. "I know you can do it."
7. "No."
8. "Let me give you my full attention."
9. "I'm sorry."
10. "Thanks, I appreciate…"

These key statements are essential to add to your dialogue because they allow your children to feel loved, validated, important, strong, capable, powerful, and that anything is possible. That they can accomplish the desires of their hearts but may not get everything they want when they want it. That as the parent, you are also human and make mistakes and you really appreciate them and their efforts. All of these phrases are life changing and assist in empowering your children and creating increased confidence and self-esteem.

So choose your words wisely and use them to empower and build up your children, not to break them down and belittle them.

Some Information Should Only Be Communicated on a Need-To-Know Basis

How much information is too much for our children? This is always something to consider as a parent. Do they need to know that we are going broke and don't have enough money to make rent this month? NO! This is TMI (too much information). Do they need to know about the problems with your love life or your parents? Do they need to know that their father or mother is a deadbeat or is not involved or supportive? NO! What benefit is it to them? None. So why share it?

There should be censor questions when deciding to share or be honest with children such as: How does it benefit them to know this information? What can they do about this? Is this age appropriate? Will knowing this information offer any value to their life? Will this information encourage them or destroy them? If there is no benefit, the news is not age-appropriate, offers your children no value, is not encouraging and they cannot do anything about it, then why share it? Why burden them with this information?

We should strive to be honest with our children, but not about everything WE KNOW. Some things are on a need-to-know basis. This is not being dishonest. It is being selective with voluntary information. They have enough to worry about with growing up. Don't add unnecessary weight to their little shoulders.

Yolandra Drake

Behavior & Discipline

"Our job is to train up a child in the way they should go."
Proverbs 22:6 New King James Version

(SECRET #16) KIDS BEHAVING BADLY IS UNIVERSAL

Do you ever wonder, "If my child's father was involved in their life, would he/she behave differently?" Do you sometimes think, "If I were still married and not a single parent, would my child be different?" Being a parent is a serious and self-sacrificial job. It is tiresome and challenging, but it can be such a wonderful and rewarding experience. I feel blessed daily that I have this amazing opportunity. Being a single parent is extremely tough and you sacrifice so much more than someone from a two parent home, but it is just as rewarding and wonderful, to say the least.

When your children do something you perceive as "out of the norm," such as habitually lying to you, sneaking out with boys or girls, constantly staying out past curfew, experimenting with smoking, drugs and alcohol, using foul language, stealing, vandalizing, performing poorly in school, acting out with you or other authority figures in their lives, etc., you may automatically attribute this behavior as defiance to your situation as a single parent. If you don't naturally think it is attributed to this, trust me, someone else is doing that thinking for you.

You may not be sure if your child is "acting out" because of your single parent situation, or if this is considered normal child or adolescent behavior. You get confused about what is considered "normal behavior" because your situation is not considered the "norm" already, so you think, "Is it because they are being raised in a single parent home?" You ask yourself, "Would this be happening if I were still married to their other parent?"

Don't Believe You are Parenting Wrong Just Because You Do it Alone

Like so many others, I asked myself those questions over and over again until I discovered the answer is undeniably YES! The secret is, it could still happen even if you are married, or with the other parent. Yes, statistics show that there is a higher incidence of acting out in single parent families, but not solely—so don't believe you are doing something wrong just because you are doing it alone.

This "acting out", mischievous type of behavior

could happen just as much in two parent households, and at times, even worse. It is universal across all economic lines, cultural and racial lines and it does not matter if there are one or two parents. These behaviors do not discriminate. Children from two parent households can be "trouble makers" involved with drugs, alcohol, gangs, prison, theft, violent acts of crime, murders, rape, low achievers, bad, unruly, or become pregnant early (as the MTV show 16 & Pregnant proves as well as the former Alaskan governor's daughter, Bristol Palin). They can be on welfare and receive government assistance as well.

Being a single parent is not easy, but it is becoming part of a more socially accepted and growing demographic (maybe because the wealthy and famous are not immune to this status). There are a lot of single parents now that are not part of these negative statistics.

Instead of demoralizing, criticizing and trying to destroy the single parent family unit, our society and communities should be attempting to educate, empower and strengthen the single parent unit so that they can be more successful. Single parent families are here to stay and will continue to grow.

Dysfunction is Present in Various Types of Families

Just because you are a single parent, does not mean that your child is destined to be a sociopath because of it. So stop believing the hype and the stereotypes or feeding into them. Don't beat yourself up or attribute your child's not-so-great behavior to only your single parent status..

The author Nancy E. Dowd (In Defense of Single Parent Families; NYU Press 1997) said it best: "Dysfunctional families come in all shapes and sizes; so do healthy families. No single form of family is essential, nor is it a guarantor of healthy, happy children." So stop beating yourself up about the dysfunction you may witness in your child or in your family and do what needs to be done to correct it and "nip it in the bud."

Today, being a single parent is a universal situation that anyone can find himself or herself in unexpectedly, and for many reasons. So those that negatively judge single parents and their children's behaviors need to not be so quick to point the finger. Adverse or bad behavior is not only prevalent in children of single parent homes but occurs in two parent, wealthy and middle class homes as well.

As single parents, be confident and know that you are OK, your kids are OK and their behavior is universal. Any child from any walk of life can have the same behavior experiences.

(SECRET #17) EITHER YOU TEACH YOUR CHILDREN—OR THE WORLD WILL TEACH THEM

We as parents are tasked with teaching our children ethics, values, positive habits and appropriate behavior. As mentioned earlier, we have to model and practice the behavior that we want our children to learn because they are watching our actions and repeat what we do. The bible says: "Train up a child in the way he should go and when he is old he will not depart from it," (Proverbs 22: 6 KJV). This refers to age appropriate discipline, which we will discuss in the next chapter.

Children are a Gift from God

Parents need to remember that God has provided the gift of children to them. Make special time with your children every day. Show them that they are loved in actions and words. Hug your children often as it supports them feeling safe, secure and loved. Play with them and get them fully engaged, guide them, provide direction, read the bible with them, pray with them, talk to them, listen to them and show them how important they are to you. A child's spiritual, emotional, mental, and physical well-being is largely determined by how they are raised.

Building positive relationships with our children is important because presenting rules without a positive relationship builds rebellion and anger. It is part of our job as parents to be actively available and learn each child's unique wiring and ways of doing things, along with that child's unique talents and gifts. Kids will most likely mimic and become what your values represent in your home. Those values will be absorbed into their lives from you and your actions in how you treat them. What do you expect from them? What behavior is simply not tolerated and non-negotiable? What you allow to happen in your home and how you speak to and treat each other is what children will see as acceptable. It is the responsibility of the parent to provide teachable moments from the time children get up until they go to sleep. This can be accomplished daily by being aware of your engagements with others as well as your children. Ensure that you are displaying in actions and words the values and ethics you hold in high regard for yourself and your family.

Initially, as a parent, we need to thoroughly do some soul searching. We need to assess and know what the values are for ourselves personally and the family. We have to ask ourselves some thought provoking questions. For example, you may ask: What things are most important to me? What are my values in life, family? What habits, ethics, behaviors and values do I want to stick with my children for the rest of their lives? What habits and values will help them be successful in this world? How can I instill these values in them starting today? Whatever these are, they need to be demonstrated whenever possible, on a daily basis. Look for ways to infuse these values and help your children learn to connect to a higher power, whatever your religious faith or choice may be. Teach them how to pray at night and begin this ritual early on.

Where Does Violent Behavior Stem From in Children?

Doing our part in trying to prevent violence and sociopathic criminal behavior within children is vital, especially in our solo parent households. Research has shown that children have a greater risk of becoming violent if they have a parent that was violent. That violence is not based on biology or inheritance of a trait, but instead it is the result of learned behavior. If there is violence and abuse in the household that children witness consistently, it will eventually negatively affect their behavior.

Violence is not relevant to demographics and has the potential to occur in single parent or two parent households. Basically, children are learning this negative behavior of violence from watching what their parents and repeating what they see. This means that violent youths are far more likely to have modeled the behavior of violent parents.

According to the Surgeon General Report of 2001, research has shown that there are: "...two proposed protective factors that seem to buffer the risk of violence and they are an intolerant attitude towards deviance and commitment to school. These two factors exert a statistically significant buffering effect on the risk of violence. An intolerant attitude toward deviance, including violent behavior, is the strongest proposed protective factor. It reflects a commitment to traditional values and norms as well as disapproval of activities that violate these norms. Young people whose attitudes are antithetical to violence are unlikely to become involved in activities that could lead to violence or to associate with peers who are delinquent or violent." So, as parents, we have to teach them values through our expectations and our actions. We have to show that we are intolerant to violence and provide children with alternatives ways to deal with their emotions and difficult situations.

How Can We Protect Our Children From Violence?

Research has also shown that violence in the media and TV shows also has an impact on promoting violence in our children. Media violence increases aggressive attitudes and emotions, which can trigger violent behavior in children. Children have access to so much media violence via games, television and the internet, coupled with large amounts of idle and unsupervised alone time to view them. Regardless of government and other interested groups' attempts to limit the amount of violence reaching American families, families themselves play a critical role in guiding what reaches their children, regardless of the family structure or demographics. It is our job as parents to limit the exposure to violence in the media that children are participating in on a daily basis. This involves active parenting: being present and aware of what your children are absorbing in their minds with TV shows, movies, video games, the internet and social media platforms. With all of the technology today, a parent's job is daunting and challenging, to say the least. We have got to find creative ways to monitor what our children are doing and watching.

The 2001 Surgeon General Report, based upon much research, concluded that there is no one factor that can predict the likelihood that a child will grow up to be violent. We, as parents, have to ensure that we are not doing things that contribute to raising violent, angry children. We must treat them fairly and not allow other adult family members or friends to treat our children in any way that violates the morals, ethics and values that we have established for our family.

We have to hold onto our children and protect them from the outside influences that are trying to manipulate our children: the influences of violence, crime, drugs, alcohol, incest, molestation, prostitution, human trafficking, teen sex and pregnancy, low self-esteem, pedophiles, and other predators and negative experiences that try to corrupt our children.. We have to give our children the tools they need to deal with these things effectively and successfully, and it starts with teaching them baseline values, habits, priorities, expectations and appropriate behavior. It is our job to protect them as much as humanly possible, and I take that job seriously.

(SECRET #18) CHILDREN DEPEND ON YOU FOR AGE APPROPRIATE DISCIPLINE

Do you struggle with disciplining the little ones? Are you concerned, frustrated and overwhelmed with how to effectively discipline your children transitioning into the tween and teen years? Discipline is fundamental and the essence of building a stable foundation with your children. So many people miss this vital aspect of parenting and wonder why their kids have no respect for them or any other adults and authority figures that they come in contact with. Discipline needs to be started early when your children are in their toddler years; it is more difficult when it is started later in the child's life, but it is best to start no matter where you are today…better late than never.

You have to discipline your children if you want them to grow and develop into law abiding, productive, respected and successful citizens of society. You have to discipline effectively if you want your children to grow up and have the best life possible. Discipline is crucial to their growth and development and their interactions and relationships in life.. Believe it or not, our children want to be disciplined, as it provides them a sense of security. Although they may act as if they don't like it, appropriate discipline allows our children to feel safe, important, cared for and loved. Effective discipline at home is the foundation for how they will behave in the world. It all starts at home!

Not all discipline is the same. I am speaking of loving, effective, firm and consistent age-appropriate discipline that does not involve spankings, beatings and cruel and unusual punishment. Too many people grew up receiving corporal methods of discipline that were passed down from generations; this can be painful, degrading, demoralizing and, most times, this will achieve the opposite results of the intended purpose and damage children emotionally and mentally.

Most Parents Tend to Repeat How They Were Disciplined

There are many forms of appropriate discipline besides spanking and whippings. These are very violent forms of punishment and a myriad of research has shown that spankings and whippings promote violence and aggression. We must be mindful of how we were raised surfacing in our parenting styles of discipline. We tend to repeat what we learned from our past and if it was not good and toxic we have to make a concerted, conscious effort to *do* something different. If we were brutally beat as a child, we may grow up and say to ourselves, "I will never beat my kids like that," but as a learned behavior, history may repeat itself. Some parents may take the other route and say, "Well, I got my ass beat as a child, and I turned out okay." This is not acceptable. It was not OK that you had to experience it and it is not OK for your children to endure this type of aggressive behavior either. Change is possible. Make a declaration that, "The change starts today!" Do something different. You don't have to repeat the past, but learn from it.

You have to first make a decision that you are going to do something different and then, like the Nike ad states, "Just Do It." It will be difficult initially because your instinctive reactions are different and imprinted from many years of training, but you have to be conscientious of your actions and intentional—don't just REACT.

You are deciding to discover, explore and utilize another form of discipline.

There are other more effective forms of disciplining your children, you just have to research, experiment and find what works best for your child or children, because they might be different for different personalities.

10 powerful tactics for effective discipline include:

1. Communication, communication, communication! Setting rules including house rules (such as how we treat and speak to each other, no hitting or yelling, etc.), boundaries and expectations. It's important to do this step first, early on.

2. Consequences established that will be the result of not abiding by the rules, and communicating these with your children so they know the rules, expectations and consequences for breaking rules. This includes natural consequences as well so they know and understand why certain rules are important (such as not hitting others because they hit back or not taking your toys to school because you might lose them).

3. Allowing them to learn to make choices to either "do this or that" based upon the information you discussed including rules, boundaries, common sense, etc. Reminding them that it is a choice and they get to decide. Teaches decision-making skills that benefit them throughout life and they learn about consequences of choices and actions.

4. Following through on the consequences you have set and discussed as well as allowing them to experience natural consequences of their actions within reason and safety. It is imperative to follow through and be consistent no matter what because you will be tested on this step especially in the beginning until your children learn you mean business. It is all a part of learning to follow the rules and if not then this is what will happen.

5. Praising them for being obedient, respectful of you as the parent and following the rules and expectations. Children need to know when they are doing well and you are noticing their efforts and appreciate them. Don't just acknowledge them when they are being disobedient, but offer praise and encouragement for continuing to perform the expected behavior because it is awe-

some and they are wonderful and you are pleased. This teaches them about mutual respect.

6. Time out as a consequence of inappropriate behavior works really well in younger children starting as a toddler and up (we'll discuss this in greater detail later).

7. Loss of privileges especially with older children and teens. This can be very effective and is tied-in with initially discussing rules/expectations and loss of privileges as a consequence of not abiding by rules and/or breaking set boundaries.

8. Giving your child "the look" that they grow to understand means they need to stop their inappropriate behavior or they are in big trouble.

9. Stern, serious tone of voice that is firm and direct and means: "I am not kidding, you need to stop it now." This works very well also with "the look" and can be used even in toddlers; it is best when started early in age. They are used to hearing your voice and can tell that it is no longer the nice playful voice, but the serious one. This works well when giving instructions and they are violating a rule and are about to be placed in timeout or suffer other consequences.

10. Consistency is critical to any type of discipline or game plan that you enforce. If you are not consistent then you will fail because your children will not trust that the rules are important enough for you to follow through on them—so why should they care and make them important to themselves? If you need to change a rule to ensure it is viable and appropriate, then do so, communicate it, but stay with the process so they respect the process. Remember they are always watching what you do. You can be flexible at times, but you have to stay consistent.

These discipline tactics make up the basic foundation for a discipline game plan that promotes respect for each other, has everyone involved in the process so that there are no surprises, and promotes responsibility, empowerment and accountability so that everyone is doing their part. You don't have to be yelling and screaming, just make sure that you are consistent and following through so they know you mean business. You decide what works best experiment with a few until you find the right fit for your children. Sometimes, you may find yourself yelling and screaming, but you can stop, re-group, calm down and use whichever tactic you have. Find what works best for your child and experiment until you find the right combination of options.

Various Discipline Methods

When my daughter was very young, I started her with timeouts. The timeouts were extremely effective for us because it provided an opportunity for her to calm down, as well as for me to calm down. I have learned even from my own personal experiences that when people spank their kids they go overboard and to unintended extremes because they usually end up taking all of their pent-up anger and aggression out on the child. Spanking in the heat of the moment can go much farther than initially intended, even for a minor discretion. Nowadays, it is also considered child abuse and you as a parent or caregiver can go to jail for it. So find alternative, effective means of discipline for both your benefit and the benefit of your child.

I grew up receiving many spankings as a child and some were extreme. I made a promise that I would never treat my child in that manner because I always felt that it was so unloving and cruel. I could not imagine how someone that loved you would treat you in that manner and state that they did it *because* they loved you. I did not understand this when I was a child, but later learned that they were doing the best they could with the limited information that was available; they had been disciplined in even worse forms. It was a family pattern; a learned behavior that had been passed on from previous generations.

I made it my mission to try and find alternative methods of discipline. This was a life changing decision. I read countless books on discipline and effective parenting methods and tried many alternative strategies. After making the decision to do something different with disciplining my child and taking the time to research, this is how I found out about an effective method called "Timeout".

Timeout Can Be Effective if Done Right

Timeout begins with first finding an appropriate timeout spot in your house either in the kitchen, living room, hallway or dining room. You explain to your child what the rules and expectations are, show them the timeout area and explain the purpose. You let them know that they will receive a warning about their behavior, and if they continue, then they will go into the timeout spot.

A good rule of thumb is one minute for every one year of age. For example, if the child is four years old, then four minutes of timeout is adequate (four minutes seems like forever to a four year old). You have to teach them to stay in the spot for the allotted amount of time by setting a timer. When the time is up, they then have to apologize for the behavior that got them into the timeout spot. They have to serve the full time. They are not allowed to talk to you or anyone else or play while in this timeout session.

Timeout is not as effective in their bedroom until they are older when they can be told not to play with their toys, computers, etc. and they will usually fall asleep, especially if they are already sleepy. Sometimes being sleepy and tired is what is causing the negative behavior in the first place. Remember, timeout is for them to calm down and for you to calm down, too, if necessary.

This will not come easily for some kids at first, but you have to be consistent. It may not come easily for the parent either at first because you have to teach the kid to stay there. It is a learning process for both. Timeout teaches them to notice and recognize their inappropriate behavior. They have to know what they did wrong. It also teaches them that there are always consequences to their actions. They also learn to acknowledge their wrongdoing and apologize for their disrespect of the rules or their negative behavior.

Once this timeout strategy is learned properly and being used consistently it can be extremely effective. My daughter was a busybody and did not like being away from the action, even for a few minutes, and timeout worked well for her. When her friends would come to visit and they were irritable, sleepy and/or fussing and fighting with each other, they all would be placed in timeout in opposite ends of the room. It worked wonders; they would calm down, apologize and go back to playing respectfully. If it happened again, back to timeout they would go. Sometimes they would fall asleep because they were tired. You have to remember the time limits appropriate for their ages and let them know when it is over, no matter how peaceful it seems; unless they are asleep, then leave them be. I will confess that I did forget a few times and found my daughter sound asleep. This happens when they are just tired, anyway.

Spankings

I must, in all transparency, truthfully and regretfully disclose that when my daughter was about six years of age, I slipped and was guilty of dishing out one or two spankings that left me feeling cruel and hypocritical. One spanking was with my hand to her butt and another with a belt to her butt with three swipes. She was devastated and confused and I am sure she questioned how someone who loved her could treat her this way. It was definitely a shocker to her (and to me) because I told myself that I would never spank my child. I did not want it to get out of hand like a few experiences in my childhood.

I noticed at both times of this happening that I was mostly angry about other things, other stressors in my life that I was dealing with. I exploded and she became the trigger and the recipient of those pent-up negative emotions; she did not deserve this. It is difficult to separate other stressors that are already on you, especially as a single parent and the normal stressors from children not being obedient. So it is best not to get into this form of discipline. Nothing my daughter did was deserving of a spanking, especially when there are other forms of discipline available. I vowed to myself that I would never spank her again, and I never did.

I will say that after receiving a couple of spankings, she never wanted to feel that again, but I knew that if I continued spankings, it would promote fear in her, and I did not want her to fear me. Some people think that their children should fear them as part of disciplining, but fear does not mean discipline or that your child is learning something. It just means that they fear you as a parent and will not want to share anything with you that may lead to a spanking/beating. When they have done something wrong, they will fear coming to you for assistance. They will fear you so much that they will try to be "perfect" and not make any mistakes, so they will not want to try new things. This leads to other problems with perfection as they grow older, because no one is perfect! Their fear can also lead to them still having mischievous behavior, but making sure by any means necessary to not get caught. This fear can also get so intense that they want to take out revenge on you or others.

You may not agree with me, but research has shown that violent behavior as discipline leads to violent, aggressive behavior in our children. There are a lot of children that grew up and became successful after receiving beatings as a child, and there are a lot that did not and ended up as sociopaths with violent, aggressive behavior and a life in prison.

I know what some people are saying and thinking: "Well, I received spankings and I turned out OK", or "Some kids need their ass beat; that is the problem with kids today." I have heard many remarks such as these to justify spankings, but they are just examples of learned, repeated behavior and there is no justification for beating a child. It is wrong and no one deserves to be treated like this. Just because you endured this type of treatment does not mean it was appropriate. It is just learned behavior passed on from generation to generation, and we all know where this type of aggressive behavior originated.

I hated spankings/beatings when I was a child, and as an adult looking back, I truly believe that most times they were extreme and did nothing but promote fear and a people-pleasing perfectionist demeanor of trying to do everything right to prevent another spanking or a beatdown. Some people go to extremes with so-called "spankings" that turn into beatings with belt buckles, brooms, shoes, extension cords, etc. No matter how you look at it, this is cruel and horrible treatment for a child to endure and can cause excessive damage physically as well as mentally and emotionally to children. Not to mention how it can be exaggerated and taken sometimes to unplanned extremes. It also promotes violence and aggressive abusive behavior in children towards themselves, their siblings, other children they come in contact with and maybe even their own parents in moments of revenge. Remember that children learn from watching what they see you do and will repeat the behavior at some point.

"The Look"

A learned tactic I started early on with my daughter was giving her "the look", which refers to my look of disappointment. I grew up receiving it from my mother. I knew as a child that when I got this look when we were in public and I was being unruly, I needed to stop it immediately or suffer the consequences when I got home. I would also get a pinch to my skin at times to get my attention if I was not aware, so that I could see the look. This is something that I learned to be effective with my daughter; I would give her my look of disappointment and she knew that it was time to straighten up or she would be in trouble, like timeout when we returned home. This is something that my other friends find effective in parenting.

Timeout was my preferred method of discipline. It worked very well and stayed in place for many years in my house until my daughter entered junior high; then I had to add taking away privileges such as cell phone, use of computer, going out, hanging out with friends, etc. You thought the "terrible twos" were challenging? Just wait until your child enters their teen years; that's when the challenge really becomes interesting because you both are continually changing.

Let Your Children Know Your Expectations

Children of every age need guidance, consistent routine, schedules, expectations, and age appropriate chores. Part of discipline involves setting and maintaining routines such as bedtime and awakening times to help children feel secure and know what to expect daily. Make sure they have at least ten hours of sleep each night. Children need more rest than adults to keep their minds alert, balanced, and functioning properly. Getting children to sleep early gives the parent alone, kid-free time to decompress, which is essential every night.

When you discipline your children, set standards and expectations at a young age and keep them consistent. This is a critical step in your discipline program and plan of action. This allows your children to grow up knowing what your standards and expectations are of them as a child/teen, family member and citizen in the community. You help mold your children; they are who they are, but you help them with basic foundational stuff.

Children Need Age Appropriate Chores

Promote healthy habits as well early on by allowing them to participate in the maintenance of the household and keeping it clean by assigning them age appropriate chores. There is something that every child can do to contribute in household chores and maintenance—yes, even starting as early as two years of age with picking up toys and placing them in bins. Starting these things as early as possible contributes to building self-esteem, independence and responsibility.

Teach and expect your children to make their beds, clean up their rooms, put away toys, organize, sweep, assist with laundry, wash dishes, set and wipe the table, clean the bathroom, take out trash, and other household duties as age appropriate. Children learning to do chores and how to gradually manage responsibilities will pay off in the future, as they get older.

When my daughter attended college I was amazed at how many of her friends knew nothing about cleaning, doing their laundry or even cooking a simple meal. These kids were from two parent households and were in college, but clueless about how to care for themselves and clean up after themselves and their surroundings in ways that did not impede upon their roommates. They were used to having someone else do it for them, either mom or a housekeeper—yes, a housekeeper cleaning their rooms for them. They had no sense of responsibility or accountability regarding cleaning up after themselves in a shared common area. They were used to someone else doing it for them and really expected it, although they did not bring the housekeeper with them.

Anecdotally, I have noticed that most of the single parents that I know have children that seem to be more independent and able to care of themselves.. A reason for this may be because more is expected from them at an early age as far as contributing to the maintenance of the home; this teaches them independence and responsibility early on. In some cases, it might also be that families with two contributing parents are more able to afford maids and cleaning services.

Be prepared for your children's excuses for not getting things done. They will always use the infamous line that kids use: "I forgot." When I began hearing this repetitive phrase one too many times, I decided to make my daughter a checklist of what was expected from her on a daily basis, from basic self-care (brushing her teeth at night, taking a shower and putting on lotions, etc.) to chores (making her bed in the morning, tidying up her room at night, preparing her clothes and backpack for the next morning, completing her homework, etc.). I even included timeframes specifying a.m. tasks and chores versus p.m. tasks and chores so that she could check off the tasks that she completed. My requirement was that I had to sign off at the end of the day and if she forgot to let me sign off and chores were not completed at the end of the week, then that was money off of her allowance. This checklist was also tied to privileges that she wanted. She was held accountable and had consequences if she did not perform her expected duties. This helped to prevent the "I forgot" statement. Because if she forgot to do anything, then I forgot to provide her the privilege that she wanted or event she wanted to attend; I also decreased her allowance. This proved to be a very effective tool, especially after she began to feel the consequences of her initial resistance and realized that I was consistent and the checklist was here to stay.

As children begin to remember their chores and expectations consistently over time and it becomes a habit, the checklist can be phased out and brought back again as needed. This tool can be useful for children that are capable of reading from school age to high school years with age appropriate expectations (I have attached a copy as a resource tool at the back of the book).

Raising Daughters is Different than Raising Sons

A question that I have been asked many times is: "You raised a daughter and I know it was challenging, especially as a single parent, but how would you have raised a son? Would it have been different?" My answer to that question is, "I was tough with my daughter but I would have been even tougher with my son." All too often, I witness women raising their sons differently than their girls-with less expectations (i.e.: letting the son be the baby of the family). The girls are raised tougher, stricter and the sons are seen as "momma's little man" with more leniencies and can do no wrong. The sons get away with murder, are sometimes more selfish, too emotional, and not raised to be strong, respectful of women and independent.

In some families, the boys may grow up weaker than the girls and with a sense of entitlement, especially with women they meet. This is not teaching them how to be strong men. From my own observations and from talking with other women raising sons, they realize they are unintentionally hurting their sons and weakening their future family unit when they do this. These sons eventually grow up and expect to be treated like "momma's little boy", be taken care of, do whatever they want and treat people in any manner they want and have a difficult time adjusting because *most* women are not going to buy into this type of treatment. In the real world, they will not be treated in the manner they are accustomed to from their moms. Stronger women will expect more from them; to be a strong man and to take care of not only themselves, but also the family.

So the answer to that question is that I would definitely be tougher with my sons. I would make sure that I am consistent with rules and consequences of their actions. I would not be easy on them because they don't have a father around; this just cripples them, as the world is not going to be more understanding or easier on them because of this. When you are too easy-going on boys or give them a pass because of an absent father or any other reason, it just promotes them using this as an excuse throughout their lives and not living up to their full potential. We have to stop doing this to our children, especially our boys. We have to stop feeding them excuses and providing them with handicaps to not live full, productive lives. I would be more of a drill sergeant with my sons, pushing them to be their best, to be strong and courageous, having respect for themselves and others, especially women. I would teach them how to have boundaries, follow rules, and teach them that there will always be consequences for their actions. I would teach them how to make decisions and how to treat women by teaching them how to respect and treat me as the first woman in their life.

Yes, I would be somewhat different in how I raise a son versus a daughter, but my discipline would be the same. I would still follow the same basic principles as outlined above (and in the Teen Discipline section to follow) until I figured out what works best. I would start out early, keeping in the forefront of my mind that in the absence of his father, it is my duty and responsibility to teach him how to be a man by any means necessary and make sure that I find mentors/role models that can reinforce and assist me in obtaining this goal that is vital for his success.

Teen Discipline

Discipline as a parent can be tough and it is even tougher as a single parent because you have to be present to discipline, and you have no one to share the responsibility with. You have to sacrifice evenings out or getting away to enforce the rules and make sure they are being adhered to. Yes, you sacrifice double as a single parent!

You have to be present to low-key spy on your kids. I know you are thinking spying on your kids is wrong, but these days, especially with so much technology out there, predators are lurking around everywhere to entice your kids with so many negative vices in the world.

I believe it is our job as parents to protect our children by any means necessary. They are not going to tell you everything no matter how close you are. You are lucky if they tell you half of the things that are going on in their lives, even if you are a "cool mom". There is always some point in their life—usually during their teens—when they will strive to be more secretive. They will unintentionally hurt you when you discover a few lies here and there and will attempt to pull away from you no matter how close of a relationship you have or how cool of a parent you think you are.

You are still "the parent". It will happen, so be ready. This is the time that you will have to get creative and turn into a spy or "detective" with a mission to stay on top of things and save your child from the temptations and people of the world that are trying to steal, rob and kill the innocence from your children. You have to say "not on my watch" and make it your mission to protect them during these tempting teen years.

No one is perfect, so no matter what you do, a few things will still get past you. Don't be discouraged. I still feel that I immobilized and prevented the "Big Ones" from coming to fruition. Yes, I would sneak into my daughter's room at night while she was sleeping and read her text messages. She was not allowed to have password protection while in junior high and high school; these were my rules, with my phone. I read some things I did not want to know, but needed to know. It was not every day, but it was consistently when I got an instinct or a nudge from God that something was going on that I needed to know—especially when I felt she was shutting down, shutting me out, she wasn't talking and I felt something was not right. It was always the right time because usually something was going on where I needed to intervene. My instincts were always right. If you pay attention to your kids, you will notice the difference in their actions—or inactions.

There were always consequences. Either she was going on punishment: cell phone was being taken away and/or we needed to have a serious talk, where I usually got her to confess and provide more information and details with stern pressure. I always knew when she was being dishonest, or holding back information. I would say, "There is something that you are not telling me and now is the time." I would act as if I knew something more, even if I knew only a little. She would eventually feel bad and would confess her mischiefs or intended mischiefs and I would discover so much more than I originally thought. The year she turned 17 was the most challenging year. She was tall, beautiful, smart and virtuous, and the boys were after her.

This is where the phrase "It takes a village" really continues to be relevant. You need a community of eyes and ears watching what the teens are up to. Thankfully, my mom visited us often and usually stayed for about 2-3 months at a time. This was extremely beneficial to me, but my daughter hated it because she had another set of eyes and ears watching her.

As the solo parent, it is your responsibility to set boundaries for your children, especially for your teenagers. They are too young to make these boundary decisions for themselves and boundaries help keep them safer, in less trouble, away from places and situations they don't need to be in or are not mature enough to handle yet.

Boundaries help decrease chances of something shady happening.

Top 4 Major Components of an Effective Discipline Game Plan with Teens

#1: Communication and establishing rules, boundaries and expectations should always be the first step in developing an action plan for effectively disciplining your children. It is critical to establish these rules, boundaries and expectations early on so it is not a shock to your child when all of a sudden you want to make this change. If not done early then better late than never, but do expect resistance if done later on. If you start early, your teen will already know how you are and what you expect from them. They may still resist, but will know it is something that they have to deal with and the resistance will be much less. Part of this establishing of rules and expectations is to have a conversation with your children about what the rules are so there is no misunderstanding.

#2: After discussing these rules, boundaries and expectations with your children, you need to establish and communicate what the consequences will be if these rules are not abided by. This allows for no surprises and ensures everyone is on the same page. This also allows them to have all of the necessary information to make informed decisions and choose to either abide by the rules or break them and suffer the consequences.

#3: The third step is to now wait to see what decision they will make. There is no need for nagging or complaining, just wait. Allow them the independence to work it out and decide what to do. When your children are younger you may want to help them with the decision and ask, "Do you want to do this as I have asked you to do, or do you want to do this and suffer this consequence? The choice is yours, you get to decide, what do you choose?"

When your children are teenagers, you have already done your part by establishing the rules and expectations as well as what the consequences will be depending on their decision. We hope they will choose wisely but it is now in their hands and their choice to make. Sometimes children especially teenagers don't mind suffering the consequences depending on how stringent they are. Sometimes they may just test you as they frequently do to see if you will follow through or if you are "just talking".

Whatever the case may be, let them learn to make their own decisions in this structured environment and learn from these decisions because this will be a valuable lesson that you are teaching them. Preparing them for their future and the real world where they will always have to make decisions and may not have anyone to help them choose wisely. If they are allowed to make decisions and suffer the consequences (good or bad) of those decisions, then they will have experience and can make wiser choices as they grow older. No matter what, you will be teaching them that choices have consequences and to weigh and consider them accordingly.

#4: The fourth and final step of this specific disciplinary game plan is to follow through on the consequences if they choose to violate the rule or expectation that you have established with them. This step is critical because you are teaching whether or not you are a woman of your word. You are teaching them whether or not they will respect you as a parent or continue to violate your rules. This final step will show them you mean business and you will always be consistent and follow through. This step is critical and needs to be consistently performed every time. Also a part of this final step is also acknowledging and praising their positive behavior when they are abiding by your rules and expectations. They need to know that you are pleased and that you notice when they are cooperating and doing their part by doing what is expected of them. They need to have attention and recognition when they are performing well, not only when they are being disobedient. This makes them feel appreciated, reinforces positive behavior and generates respect.

These steps are fundamental to effective discipline—especially with teens—and have to be practiced over and over again. They also have to be tweaked and rules need to be renegotiated as appropriate throughout your child's developmental stages.

Do You Know Where Your Teens Are?

Yes, you need to know where your children and teenagers are throughout the day and evening. It does not mean that you don't trust them, but that you love and care about them. If something were to happen, you need to know their whereabouts. Teens are not adults and they need to keep you informed because you are the adult in the family, responsible for their well-being as a parent. I am amazed when I talk with parents that have no idea where their children or teens are and who they are hanging out with. As the comedian Steve Harvey says, "You got to know what your kids are doing or else your kids are going to do you."

Create an atmosphere of open communication with established family times and routines and try, if at all possible, for everyone to eat dinner together most evenings. This can be a great time to connect with your teens during meals. Don't force the conversation though. I have learned from experience that right after school was the worst time for effective communication with my daughter, especially as a teen. My daughter was always vague with answers when I asked, "So how was your day?" She would respond with one or two words and I would get so frustrated because she is usually a talker. I had to learn that just as I am moody and not in a talkative, sharing mood all the time, the same applied to her and I had to respect that. I began to notice that after she had the opportunity to unwind and get settled around dinner, she was in a talkative mood and eager to share the events of the day non-stop and unsolicited. You just have to learn your children and their timing and not force communication and bonding when they're not in the mood. They don't mean any harm or ill will towards you; it's not personal, and they are just being human. Keep being present and it will happen.

Respect Each Other

Give respect to each other. Speak with respect to your kids and demand that they respect you in return. You cannot be yelling and cussing at your children and expect them to respect you. Remember, respect is earned. It goes both ways and your children will do as you do.

Schedule regular family meetings that can also be held around dinner to discuss important issues, schedules, and activities. Dinner was a great time that worked in my household; choose a time that is convenient for your family, maybe even right after dinner. This "meeting" is also a great time to discuss new rules or changes in rules and other expectations and boundaries. Let it be a discussion so that your children can negotiate with you and you are compromising so they feel heard and understood. They may have some valid issues, concerns or arguments to make that may be beneficial to both sides. Just be open to hearing them!

Every Conversation Cannot be a Lecture

An important communication skill that I am still working on with my daughter is to remember to not turn every conversation into a lecture. Children are lectured at school all day, every day. The last thing they need is to come home and hear more from you, the parent. I have learned there is an extremely fine line between giving advice and lecturing so we as parents must try our best not to get them confused. Advice is usually solicited and suggestive and lecturing is constant and unsolicited—telling a person what they should do, how they should do it, and when.

Along with not lecturing, also avoid the temptation of constantly repeating what you say over and over again, at least not in the same conversation. I am a huge believer that consistent communication, especially of important messages that you want your children/teens to digest and stick with, need to be repeated periodically, just not in the same conversation. Constantly repeating the same thing over more than twice is really about control and your teens will begin to tune you out. Say what you mean, mean what you say and get to the point, because you will be wasting your time and speech on deaf ears after too long.

Choose Your Battles

Another huge lesson that I have learned with disciplining my daughter at every age (but especially in the teen years and now college) is to choose my battles. When you are parenting teenagers, not everything needs to be a fight, lecture or battle. This can be exhausting and non-productive and create animosity and tension if you make a mountain out of every molehill. Instead of getting angry with every issue, think about it and decide if it is a priority and just ask, "Why did this happen?" or "Why was this not done?" Give them an opportunity to explain. If they don't want to talk about it in detail and if it is really not that important, let it go. It will save you both grievances over something that is insignificant. "Don't sweat the small stuff."

You also *need* to know the parents of the children that your kids hang out with and their addresses and phone numbers, as well as their friends' phone numbers.

This is a must! You don't have to be best friends with the parents; you just need to communicate with them when the kiddos have plans to go shopping, to play games, or have sleepovers and parties to make sure everything is legitimate. Your child may say, "My friend so-and-so's mom/dad does not ask all these questions or have to get phone numbers or call the other parents to confirm plans," and you have to remind them that things are done differently in your house and this is the expectation so they can either get with the program or stay home.

Remember they are going to always challenge you and you want them to (in an appropriate manner) because this helps them communicate their ideas effectively with others as they grow up.

Children of all ages will challenge you to see how you will respond. You have to stay consistent and let them know you are paying attention to everything. I used to tell my daughter, "Everything done in the dark will be come to light and be revealed, and I will eventually find out." The ironic thing is that most times I did find out, or she would eventually tell on herself. This paraphrased quote was learned during my childhood based on biblical teachings from Luke 8:17 NKJV: "For nothing is secret that will not be revealed, nor anything hidden that will not be known and come to light." Life experiences have made me a firm believer of this and I have been a witness to it time and time again.

Single Parents Have to Pay Attention and Be Nosey

You have to stay engaged and be present, always asking questions—even the uncomfortable ones. When you get lazy and stop paying attention, your teens will notice and feel they have worn you down and will be victorious and will start to play all types of games because they know you are not paying attention. This is the worst thing you can do for your child and at the most critical time of their lives.

You have to make consequences for unacceptable behavior and let your child/teen know ahead of time what the expectations are and what the consequences are for not following your rules. Then you have to stick to the consequences no matter what. If they commit the crime, they have to do the time. Teach them this lesson early on because society will not give them breaks and will not be lenient on them. Our children have to learn the consequences of their actions and the preferred place to learn this is at home.

As my daughter was growing up and making new friends, I felt it was important to make our home kid/teen friendly so that my daughter and her friends desired to hang out at our house. This provided me the opportunity to get to know her friends and they got to know me as well as my expectations and what kind of parent I was. I made sure there were games, music and food in the house and they had a place they could feel comfortable. I always liked her friends for the most part, but there were a few that were a little sketchy and they did not last long.

The sketchy ones always tried to avoid me, avoided eye contact and usually were not as friendly and wanted to keep away from me. These are the type of friends you want to keep an eye on because they are trying to undermine you with your child when you are not present. Stay strong and stay present and they will soon know that you are on to them and they will soon move on.

Your child will eventually sense a friend's negative presence as well, especially with you shining the spotlight on their sketchy behavior at appropriate times during conversation. Teen years are when your children need you more than ever. You have to be tough as a parent. You cannot be weak. Don't get weary or give up now. You have come too far. This is when you need your support system to talk with you, bless you, encourage you and uplift you so you can continue the good fight for your children.

There are many negative vices in the world fighting hard to get your child and take them away from you spiritually, physically, emotionally and mentally. This will be the most difficult time. It is the final stage of parenting your child to successfully becoming a young adult and a respected and law-abiding citizen of the community. Get re-energized and get back into the fight. You CAN DO IT! You have to "JUST DO IT" (as Nike says)! Your teens are depending on you.

EDUCATION

(SECRET #19) LOVE AND APPRECIATION OF SCHOOL/ EDUCATION STARTS AT HOME WITH THE PARENT

Developing a love and/or appreciation of education starts with "YOU" as the parent. You are your child's first teacher and mentor. Teaching children the importance and value of education is extremely significant and is the foundation that you want to begin to build from infancy. Yes, infancy. Even while your baby is inside of the womb. You can begin this process by reading to your child on a daily basis or as much as possible at this early stage.

Kids will develop a love for learning and reading depending on the emphasis that you place on it. We as parents set the standards for our children early on because children repeat what we do and will try to meet our expectations, but we have to provide those expectations first. We help to create their interests. If we want them to be avid readers and love books it is important that they see us being avid readers and reading to them, even daily if possible. They will begin to love the sounds of words and stories that those words create, by the emphasis and inflection in your voice that you place on those words and sounds. With consistency on a daily basis, you are developing rituals and routines around reading. This will encourage them to try to emulate you and tell stories as you do and learn to read and pretend to read their favorite stories that they have heard you repeat many times. It is remarkable and so enjoyable to watch this process develop. Encourage your child's attempts at reading even when they don't really know how. This will foster the drive to want to learn and they will be eager both in class and at home.

Reading to your children regularly and making sure you set aside even a small amount of time to read a quick book or two a day will pay off tremendously. If it is important to you, then it becomes important to them. Plus, it provides an excellent opportunity to develop these rituals and traditions early on; something that they can depend on to always be there. It is calming, a time to share quality time, and a great way to unwind after a busy day and settle down together.

Make Reading a Bedtime Ritual

Any time that you read to your children is great, but it is especially gratifying to include reading as a bedtime ritual. This can help them get to bed easier because it offers something to look forward to. It also provides the opportunity for them to quiet down, and it promotes cuddling time and closeness with your kids, building intimacy, love of reading and rituals at the same time. This might also be a time when your child is comfortable enough to share something important that they were unable to share earlier when everyone was so distracted and hectic because it is now a different, more serene atmosphere.

Allow your child to select at least one book and make one or two a favorite nighttime reading ritual that they will always remember. This is a book they can save and pass on to their children. My daughter looked forward to the bedtime ritual of reading which always included one of her all-time favorite books, "Time for Bed" by Mem Fox. No matter what, it was the last book read every single night.

Are your children excited about reading? My daughter was excited to learn how to read and began practicing reading stories to me because it made her feel more mature and even loving because she was emulating my actions. She knew I did this for her and she enjoyed it and now she wanted to share this same joy and gift with me. She would say, "Mom it is my turn to read to you tonight," and would use the same inflections in her voice and attempt to read it in the exact same manner that I read to her. Even before she knew how to completely read, she memorized the stories and knew what the basic story pattern was. She would improvise some of the wording, imitating my manner of reading to her. It was so much fun and she was improving her memory skills, public speaking skills, confidence, and desire and passion to read.

Early Education is Critical

Begin early education with your children by enrolling them in preschool and early education classes. This benefits them educationally, but also socially as they learn to interact and socialize with other children and adults in a positive manner. The sooner your child is exposed to education and the educational system, the better for them and their learning curve. It is also sending an important foundational message regarding the importance of education to your children.

Choose your child's school—including daycare—carefully. Most single parents (at least those I know personally) don't have the luxury of keeping their children at home until preschool or first grade and have to enroll their babies in a good childcare program as an infant. This means that you have to do your research on the childcare facility and make sure that it is licensed, accredited, and you have heard great reviews or received a referral from someone that you know and trust their judgment and their parenting style and expectations are similar. There are a lot of great childcare programs out there but all are not accredited. When they are licensed they meet minimum standards that are set to provide greater assurance that your children are in a safe environment with appropriate background checks and safeguards in place to provide greater security and protection for your prized possessions.

Search for information regarding the potential schools on the internet. The internet is a great resource for researching and finding information regarding reviews of the school, their ratings, if they are licensed and accredited, and if there are any complaints on the internet or with the Better Business Bureau.

Thoroughly Check Out and Question Childcare Providers

Interview the director of the school and meet the teachers or childcare providers that will be caring for your children. Make a list of essential questions that you need to have answered such as: How long have they been in business? What is their method of discipline? How do they report the daily progress and activities of your child? Is the caregiver consistent? What are the requirements of the staff that they hire? Do they conduct background checks for their employees? What is the childcare provider to children ratio? Ask any pertinent questions that you can think of. Write them down so you don't forget what to ask. This interview is critical and will help you decide the best childcare facility for your child.

This process is repeated again for preschool.

Setting Expectations and Tips for Schools:

As children grow up, they need to know what the expectations are for school, starting from day one. These include good behavior in school, respect towards their teachers, other adults and their classmates, as well as following the rules. They need to know that you expect nothing but their best academically and for them to work hard and have a good work ethic.

You will learn early on what type of student your child is and what their personal best is. Everyone's best is different and you as a parent have to learn, respect and appreciate your individual child's best and encourage it. There may be five different children in the household and each child will have their own personal best in learning and education and even sports and musical creative skills. You cannot impose one child's best onto another one. They have to be treated as individuals in this regard because that's what they are. Some will be quick learners, while others will require a little more time and patience.

Pay attention as a parent, talk with their teachers and learn your child's learning style early on. This strategy can save yourself and your child from unnecessary frustration and also help you support them in the ways they need to be supported while accepting their differences and sending the supportive message that you acknowledge them and their uniqueness.

I knew early on that my daughter was an excessive "talker" and was "extremely social." Starting in preschool her reports were always: "she is smart, does great in class, gets along well with others, but is too talkative and social during class." I also learned that my daughter could naturally get A's and B's without putting much studying and effort in, so I made sure to keep her engaged in K-level, honors and higher level classes because she could handle them. My challenge was getting her to do better and get as many A's as she could, which would require more effort. I did this only because I knew she could improve and I wanted her to strive for her best. I let her know that "this is an A and B house"—no C's or less were acceptable. This was the standard and the expectations were set early on to excel. You have to set the standards and expectations in your household to provide children structure and goals to strive for.

My daughter received her first and only "C" in high school and her most prized privileges were revoked until she brought her grade up. This was not because I am a perfectionist, (far from it); no, this was only because I knew she could perform better if she applied herself more. I wanted her to know I would not accept mediocrity from her and did not want her to settle for mediocrity herself, but to push herself to strive for her personal best. That is how you compete in the world, in life. That is how you learn success, by striving for it and not settling for less than your best. Being average and accepting being average when you know you can do better is not striving for your best and it promotes laziness. I was not aspiring to raise a lazy child.

Now don't get me wrong, I can hear some critics saying now that a "C" does not always mean mediocrity, but for her it did because I knew as an involved parent without a doubt that she could do better. Also, a grade of "C" translates to an average grade, no matter how you analyze it. She was just getting by and testing to see if she could get away with it. If I had known that she had given her best and received a "C" then I would have accepted it as her best and been proud of her. We would have celebrated, but I knew otherwise, and she was honest and also admitted to knowing that she did not perform her best and should have done better.

Support Children with Tutoring if They Need It

If you feel that your kids need a tutor, then you must definitely by all means get them a tutor. Assistance is, however, always available for free at their schools. I discovered that teachers offer tutoring and review sessions and assistance with their students after school and sometimes before school. I encourage you to make sure that your child signs up for this extra assistance whenever possible even if they feel they are doing well. This keeps them focused and up to par. If they are struggling or not, this extra attention and support will be extremely beneficial and allow them to get to know their teachers, who also know they are invested in their education and grades.

Kids want and need to have goals and standards set early in life by their parents so they can learn to set higher goals and standards for themselves later in life. Some children are naturally high achievers and are self-motivated, while others are not. Know the differences in your children and coach as necessary.

Yolandra Drake

Tips to Support Children in School

Education is vital and it is important to make sure they are in classes that sufficiently challenge them and keep them interested or they will get bored. If classes are too challenging and they do not have the acquired knowledge, skills, resources or tutoring to help them get through it then they will get distracted, unmotivated, develop feelings of being dumb, stupid, not good enough or worthy and will become bitter and frustrated. This is the recipe for downward spiraling and they can spiral out of control if no one is paying attention. It can be a breeding ground for poor, declining grades, followed by despair and loss of enthusiasm or desire to continue on.

This is when they can become distracted and begin to engage in unhealthy affiliations with others that are not doing well that they feel they connect with. There is also heightened potential at this point to become involved in gangs, theft and other negative behavior because they are losing confidence and acting out in other ways. These are extreme warning signs that they are just giving up and feel like, "If no one else cares, why should I?" How the adults in their life respond at this time will determine the path that is taken. THIS is the FORK in the road and it gets missed so much with so many kids.

Also, you have to be vigilant and try to show up to field trips or send a grandma or other family member in your place from time to time. This is where the village comes into play if you are not always available and sends a strong, positive message to the teacher that the child is loved and cared for. You and your child both benefit from it along with the other family members that can attend.

My daughter loved for either her aunt or myself to attend field trips. I made it my priority to attend as often as I could and even assisted with being a room mom at times. It took a lot of work, effort and finagling on my part, and I was grateful to have a job with a flexible schedule that allowed me these opportunities. Everyone does not have this luxury, but this is when the village steps in to help out. At times, my schedule did not allow me to attend and this is when I used my village back-up system. Send the grandparents, aunts, uncles, cousins, single friends, etc.—anyone you trust who you can enlist to help out.

I have noticed over the years that sometimes children

will get labeled as "unmotivated" or "slow learners" when in actuality they may just need a little more attention or tutoring. Maybe they missed a basic knowledge skill or step and did not get something in a prior lesson and now it has them all messed up. If the teacher does not take the time to figure this out, then the child can start this downward spiral from one missed step that was not caught because he or she did not know. It got missed and no one took the time to assess the situation. This same child starts failing and becomes unmotivated. Neither you, nor the child, have any idea what happened.

There are also times when children are in schools where they are excelling according to the standards in that particular school and district, but may still not be educationally competitive when compared with students from other privileged, more resourced school districts. This happens a lot in low income and some middle-income schools where kids are not adequately prepared. Then they enter an excelled high school or college and feel inadequate compared to the other children. They may begin to lose their confidence and feel they cannot compete, start to flunk classes or obtain lower grades and test scores than what they were used to, especially if there is not a good support system or someone that cares enough to assess the situation and offer necessary assistance to the child.

This is where really good, vigilant parenting comes into play. You cannot expect the teachers to do it for you. There are some great teachers out there, but with so many students with high teacher-student ratios, fewer resources, lower teacher pay, and less quality checkpoints in place, your child could slip through the cracks. I did not want this to happen to my child and I don't want it to happen to yours. It will take a lot more effort, especially as a single parent, but you have to find a way to stay involved consistently and get help for you and your child when it is needed throughout their school years. It is critical for their success.

Help them with their homework. Monitor their homework to ensure it is done until you trust them completely to do it alone, but make sure you still check up on them intermittently. Monitor their grades periodically. Ask them how the test went. Make it a habit and expectation that they share their graded assignments and tests with you. There are now websites for the schools and they post grades online. This allows the parents to continually stay involved in the child's progress. You are alerted when assignments are due and /or missing so that issues can be addressed promptly. Take advantage of this technology to support your children.

Benefits of Advanced and AP Level Classes

If your kids excel in class, make sure they are in the most advanced classes they can register for such as K-level and AP classes in high school. These classes are more challenging and offer higher GPA weightings for the same grade as regular classes. If the advanced classes prove to be too challenging for your child, they can always drop back down to regular level but don't allow them to do this until you have exhausted all resources to help and support them at this advanced level. Even if they make a "C" in the advanced class it is weighted higher than the regular class and considered a "B" in an on-level regular class; they just worked harder to get it and learned more advanced teachings than what they would have learned in a regular class. If it is just too tough at their best then by all means let them move back to regular classes so they don't have to struggle so much and get discouraged.

Grade reports were always a big thing in my house. Goals were set and grades were celebrated. Grandma and Aunt were also involved and periodically provided rewards for exceptional report cards. We would go out to eat and make it an event; celebrating success was huge in our house. We enjoyed celebrating small and large victories and achievements. My daughter worked hard and it was always worth celebrating. She enjoyed the celebrations because it validated her hard work and I wanted her to bask in the success of it. The impact of the celebrations has remained intact now, even in her college years, because she continues to work hard and strive for personal achievement. We still celebrate her successes.

There is no doubt that an essential aspect of healthy child development is forming a secure attachment in infancy to a parent or other adult who senses and responds to a baby's needs. Likewise, researchers agree that having a loving adult who is interested in and supportive of a child or young person's ideas and activities helps that child or adolescent develop the confidence and competence needed to progress from one stage of development to the next. Good relations with an adult who supports conventional behavior and disapproves of delinquent behavior can provide invaluable guidance for young people.

Commitment to school is a proposed protective factor that has been found to buffer the risk of youth violence. Young people who are committed to school have embraced the goals and values of an influential social institution. Such young people are unlikely to engage in violence, both because it is incompatible with their orientation and because it would jeopardize their achievement in school and their standing with adults (Jessor et al., 1995; Turbin, 2000).

Get Children Involved in Extracurricular Activities

Extracurricular activities such as art, music, drama, school publications and the like give adolescents an opportunity to participate in constructive group activities and achieve recognition for their efforts. Studies have found that recognition for or involvement in various types of activities—whether family, school, extracurricular, religious, or in the community—helps protect children from antisocial behaviors. Constructive extracurricular activities keeps children busy and can keep them out of trouble.

Children need to know that you believe in them and that they are capable. If you believe in them you empower them to learn to believe in themselves. Participating in other activities allow children to develop competence and confidence in themselves and their abilities as they discover where their strengths are and what activity they are best in as well as passionate about. You never know what you like or excel in until you try it out.

When involving children in activities, be mindful to not overwhelm them. One or two activities are good, especially to start off with. According to the American Academy of Pediatrics, unstructured playtime supports kids' social, emotional and cognitive development. It also helps them manage stress. Children need downtime just as adults do. They need time to be still sometimes and just unwind.

Be cognizant of stress and look for signs (such as irritability, frustration with doing simple tasks) that your child may be having anxiety and feeling stressed in school or extracurricular activities. If you notice unusual behavior, address it with your children and help them to communicate it so that steps can be taken to reduce the stress. Be sure to incorporate unstructured downtime into children's daily schedules.

I cannot emphasize the importance of making education a priority in your household, especially as a single parent. We all know (also from the earlier chapters) the stereotypes that are associated with single parent children, especially in regards to academic performance.

With these statistics and low expectations glaring at single parents and our children, we have to ensure that our kids don't make the stereotypes a reality. It does not have to become a reality for you or your child, but we have to do our part in ensuring that our kids defy the stereotypes…because they can! Education is vital!

(SECRET #20) SINGLE PARENTS WEAR MANY HATS

Are you concerned about what role you play in your child's life as a single parent? Do you worry about juggling and wearing so many different hats? Welcome to the club! Raising kids to be happy, healthy, positive, giving, self-confident and successful in life and relationships is extremely challenging in this day and age and even more so in a single parent household. As a single parent, you wear many hats to help facilitate healthy development of your kids.

You are your child's parent, teacher, mentor, coach, friend, confidante, playmate, etc.—especially as a single parent and more so when you have only one child. There is a fine line that you have to be sure not to cross and you have to learn how to delicately balance the relationship so that it remains healthy and functional. Everyone may not be able to handle or have an interest in this type of balance with his or her child, but it worked wonderfully for us and has kept us close throughout the years, especially through the challenging teenage years. It helped with my role as her confidante.

Confidante Hat...

Children will not tell you everything by far, but they will not confide in you at all if they don't feel they can trust you. Sometimes you have to listen not as a parent, but as a friend or confidante first, for children to trust and share pertinent information and problems with you. This will provide you the opportunity to help them explore safe options and devise appropriate solutions to their problems. Be forewarned, because sometimes, it may be too much information; something you may not want to know or may be difficult for you to hear but this comes with the territory if you want them to trust you with sacred information.

This type of trust and dialogue as a confidante and friend is crucial as your children are getting older and matriculating through junior high, high school and college where there is so much peer pressure and danger lurking. They need you to help them through this phase of life and self-discovery.

While wearing various hats, especially as the confidante, friend and playmate, it is crucial that boundary lines are adequately and clearly defined and etched in stone. This ensures your child understands them and knows that you are the parent *first* and *foremost* (especially when you have to change hats unexpectedly). The Parent Hat is the initial and most important hat you wear and the relationship that must be most respected and defined. The other roles are secondary, but also extremely relevant to fostering a loving, respectful, honest and trusting relationship between you and your children.

Do You Believe You Can Be Your Child's Friend and Parent?

As I was parenting, I always heard from others that I couldn't be my child's friend. I totally understood this perspective but did not agree wholeheartedly. Like anything in life, you have to have balance and boundaries. There is a fine line between being a parent and a friend to your child and in most situations it is your job first and foremost to be the parent first! You have to be able to not muddy the waters by trying to be a friend as well.

However, I am a firm believer that you can be your

child's friend to a certain degree as long as you maintain appropriate boundaries, which is a delicate balancing act. You have to know and learn the appropriate times to change hats between parent and friend. Don't expect to be your child's best friend when they are younger but this friendship will grow possibly into that when they are adults; they may even see you as "one of their best friends." It is a priceless, wonderful accomplishment to have sustained a relationship with your child that blossoms beautifully in adulthood. Also, don't expect to be your child's friend when you are being the disciplinarian. This is a definite no-no.

My daughter and I certainly knew without a doubt that I was the parent first, but I also wanted her to know that she could trust me and depend on me as a friend. She could share things with me and trust in me as a friend (this is when I wore my Friend Hat). I wanted her to come to me for advice, guidance, help with major decisions, disappointments, etc. I did not want her to see me as only an authoritarian, but to know that I could be both, even if not simultaneously.

The Playmate Hat: Have Fun!

When your children are younger, you will wear the hat of the playmate most often, especially if they don't have other siblings or playmates in their lives. This hat takes a lot of physical energy, and your inner child will come out to play. Children really enjoy when you interact and play with them on their level. Most times you are the person that introduces play to your child at an early age. Playtime becomes a fun ritual, so enjoy it with your child, let yourself go, play and have fun. Of course, this does not have to cease when your children are older, you just find age appropriate play with your children to make play a family ritual in your household. As they get older, have board games and family night, play card games; there is so much you can do to be one of your child's best and most fun playmates. They will love it, appreciate it and remember these fun times.

Mentors are Instrumental

As I mentioned earlier, the old saying that "it takes a

village to raise a child" is absolutely true, as long as they are positive role models and mentors. When you don't have family members as positive role models, it is extremely important to surround your children with other alternatives and mentors such as Big Brothers & Sisters organizations and social organizations (such as Girl Scouts, Boy Scouts, Jack & Jill of America, INC, school activities, clubs, great friends, Boys and Girls Clubs of America, church, etc.). It may be time-consuming to start, but will be so worth it in the end for both you and your children.

One of my daughter's friend's mother never married while her daughter was young, but she adopted a mentor from church as a surrogate father for her child during her grade school years and beyond. This seemed to work out really well for them. It was someone who she knew and trusted. You have to be extremely careful whom you allow around your children at young ages. This is when they are most vulnerable, and as we know, there are people in the world, even in our churches, that exploit and target children in these types of situations. So just be careful. It can be a great relationship to develop for your child, if chosen wisely.

Remember, you will always be one of your child's first mentors. This is one of many hats that you will wear. Wear it well!

Role Models

Friendships are extremely important in developing healthy relationships both for yourself and your kids. This is when you are wearing your "role model" hat. They need to see you in healthy relationships with friends, family, significant others, co-workers, neighbors, etc. You exemplify to your kids what that should look like and they emulate what you do. Always remember your kids are always watching what you say and do and this includes how you treat others as well as how you are being treated.

Don't let your children hear you speaking negative or gossiping about your friends, family or anyone that you have a close relationship with. They will do the same thing with their friends, family, etc. and this is a negative habit that you do not want them to engage in. It is not healthy and it disrupts them from developing trusting, intimate relationship with people. As mentioned previously, children are likely to repeat the learned behaviors they see you do.

This also means not speaking negatively about the absent mother or father in the child's presence no matter how upset or disappointed you are with the other person's behavior. This was something I learned early on. It may make you feel superior or like the "good parent" or more loving parent but this definitely is destructive to your child although self-serving for you. The other parent is technically an extension of the child; they are descendants of the other parent just as they are of you and it increases the hurt and pain for the child and makes them defensive of the other parent who is not there to defend him or herself. It is not a good look so refrain from doing it.

No matter what the situation, this will hurt your child because unconsciously they attribute the other parent to how they feel about themselves in some way. Any negative feelings you impose or suggest will stick with them and trickle into other important relationships with members of the opposite sex. This is especially true and common for girls, but also for young boys who don't have a father figure to emulate and teach them how to be a man.

Allow your children to witness you treating others, including strangers, with respect. Be mindful of modeling the behavior that you wish them to display. You will teach them how to treat you and others while wearing your role model hat.

Teaching and Coaching

The teaching and coaching hats are essential and will be adorned throughout your children's lives. These hats are worn when navigating them through life, love, how to speak up for themselves, take care of themselves, how to say NO comfortably, assisting them with education and homework, coaching them through sports, and other life-long learning skills.

There are so many hats that you will wear even beyond these mentioned. Just be flexible and consciously aware of the hat that is needed for the moment. Remember, the Parent Hat will most always be on and is the most essential, especially if you feel you cannot balance the other hats alone. Always wear the Parent Hat!

CONCLUSION

This concludes *Single Parent Secrets: How to Master Solo Parenting & Raise Amazing Children.* There are many secrets to raising children as a single mother that I have discovered over the years. I wanted to touch on these top 20 that were critical to my parenting success, laying a solid foundation to raise my wonderful daughter and become a Single Parent that Rocks!

There is no scientific formula for what will work for all kids, but I hope I have provided you great options for trial and some inspiration along the way. Take what you like and leave the rest. Strive to be the best single parent that you can be so your child is provided the maximum opportunity to thrive and live the life they ultimately deserve.

Much love and success to you and your family!

SINGLE PARENT SECRETS

SAMPLE SCHEDULE

(SAMPLE)
TO-DO SCHEDULE

Week Beginning:

	Monday	Tuesday	Wednesday	Thursday	Friday	Saturday	Sunday
A.M.	brush teeth	brush teeth	brush teeth	brush teeth	brush teeth		
	wash face	wash face	wash face	wash face	wash face		
	make bed	make bed	make bed	make bed	make bed		
P.M (afterschool)	homework	homework	homework	homework	homework		
	violin lessons		practice violin	practice violin		practice violin	practice violin
						clean bath	laundry/uniform
	p/u after self	p/u after self	p/u after self	p/u after self	p/u after self	p/u after self	p/u after self
	set clock	set clock	set clock	set clock	set clock		set clock
	brush teeth	brush teeth	brush teeth	brush teeth	brush teeth		brush teeth
	wash face	wash face	wash face	wash face	wash face		wash face
By 8pm	shower	shower	shower	shower	shower	shower	shower
Sun-Fri	lotion body /deo	lotion body /deo	lotion body/deo	lotion body /deo	lotion body /deo		lotion body / deo
	empty trash		vacuum floors	empty trash		vacuum	
	violin/backpack	violin/backpack	violin/backpack	violin/backpack	violin/backpack		violin/backpack
	at door	at door	at door	at door	at door		at door
	clothes ready	clothes ready	clothes ready	clothes ready	clothes ready		clothes ready

INSTRUCTIONS: Please check off each task as completed each day and present to me before retiring to bed Sun - Fri. Everything needs to be completed by 8pm everyday during the week except Tuesday and Thursday d/t VB

REFERENCES

U.S. Census Bureau data 2010, 2012

U.S. Department of Health and Human Services, National Center for Health Statistics, Survey on Child Health, Washington, DC, 1993.

Children's Defense Fund

Children in need: Investment Strategies...Committee for Economic Development)

FBI Law Enforcement Bulletin - Investigative Aid

Carol W. Metzler, et al. "The Social Context for Risky Sexual Behavior Among Adolescents," Journal of Behavioral Medicine 17 (1994).

Terry E. Duncan, Susan C. Duncan and Hyman Hops, "The Effects of Family Cohesiveness and Peer Encouragement on the Development of Adolescent Alcohol Use: A Cohort-Sequential Approach to the Analysis of Longitudinal Data," Journal of Studies on Alcohol 55 (1994).

Center for Disease Control, Atlanta, GA

Holy Bible: New Century Version. Copyright © 1987, 1988, 1991 by Thomas Nelson, Inc. New Century Version Online.

Holy Bible: King James Version

Deane Scott Berman, "Risk Factors Leading to Adolescent Substance Abuse," Adolescence 30 (1995)

U.S. Department of Health and Human Services, National Center for Health Statistics, Survey on Child Health, Washington, DC, 1993.

Source: Terry E. Duncan, Susan C. Duncan and Hyman Hops, "The Effects of Family Cohesiveness and Peer Encouragement on the Development of Adolescent Alcohol Use: A Cohort-Sequential Approach to the Analysis of Longitudinal Data," Journal of Studies on Alcohol 55 (1994).

Surgeon General Report of 2001

(http://www.ncbi.nlm.nih.gov/books/NBK44293/).

Jessor, R. J., van den Bos, J., Vanderryn, J., Costa, F. M., & Turbin, M. S Protective factors in adolescent problem behavior: Moderator effects and developmental change. Developmental Psychology. (1995); 31: 923–933.

ACKNOWLEDGEMENTS

Where do I begin? Completing a project like this for the first time is exhilarating but also involves a lot of work, love, encouragement, and support from wonderful people.

I give an abundance of gratitude to one of my biggest supporters, my mother Alice, my friend, my rock, my village. She has loved, supported her granddaughter and me and listened to me talk about this book for years. I thank my beautiful sister Berlando for her initial support and encouraging me to write this book since a fleeting topic in a conversation over 10 years ago. Thanks to my brother Ed, of course for keeping life interesting and other family members, friends, and acquaintances that have supported my family and me over the years.

A special recognition and thank you goes to my loving daughter Haley who has been my stimulus for living the life that created this book. She is a gift and blessing, my live muse for striving to be the best single parent that I could possibly be to enrich her life. Haley has been a cheerleader and strong supporter and also assisted with early editing and proofreading of the initial draft.

I am grateful for all my new friends in Houston who have been my village and support. I am especially thankful for and have to mention my longest and my closest friends and fellow single mothers, Rhonda, Glynis, Becky, Denean for exchanging stories, love, encouragement, and support. Thanks to one of my best friends Gretchen, who has always been there for me no matter what to love and support my daughter and me. Thanks to my good friends Andrea and Sylvia who have been surrogate aunts to my daughter since we moved to Houston. Thanks to my dearest friend Ja'Ethel, who keeps me grounded and encourages me to not let life stress me out. Thanks to my college friend and single father Tyrail, who has always provided the male perspective of single parenting while being a wonderful father.

I would like to thank my Editor, Michelle Josette. Michelle has worked with me for several months to make sure that my writing, spelling, and grammar was intact while maintaining my authentic voice and message. I thank my Coach, James Budd from Vision Fire Coaching, for helping me get clear on my vision and purpose while developing my comfort level of transparency to share my story. Also Alicia Dunmas and her Best Seller in a Weekend course for helping me complete this book and get it published. Thanks also for my great Author portrait: T.F.M. Photography Mack Taylor in Houston and Cover designer: Meela (Mila).

I also give an abundance of thanks to all of the Single Parents who are out there being AWESOME and AMAZING parents to their children and doing their personal best. You are an inspiration and I wanted to share our struggles, our challenges, joys, pains, and our truths.

Always present first and foremost in my life, I would like to give a special praise and THANKS to the MOST HIGH, my FATHER GOD, who has blessed and protected my family and I, and consistently shows me that even though I am single parent, I am never alone. HE LOVES ME and is ALWAYS WITH ME. I truly believe I was PURPOSED to write this book through HIM to service fellow Single Parents and their children.

ABOUT THE AUTHOR

Yolandra Drake is a graduate of Southern Illinois University where she received her BSN and became a registered nurse, working with adults and chronically ill children. When she became a single parent and needed more flexibility with work, she created a career pathway into pharmaceutical sales. Since then, she has been a top selling, record-breaking, multiple award-winning representative throughout her career, all while thriving as a single mom.

Yolandra currently resides in Houston, Texas and has a daughter in Law School.

Made in the USA
Columbia, SC
21 June 2017